CHINA HANDBOOK SERIES

LITERATURE AND THE ARTS

Compiled by
the *China Handbook* Editorial Committee

Translated by
Bonnie S. McDougall
and Hu Liuyu

FOREIGN LANGUAGES PRESS   BEIJING

First Edition 1983

ISBN O-8351-0989-5

Published by Foreign Languages Press
24 Baiwanzhuang Road, Beijing, China

Printed by Foreign Languages Printing House
19 West Chegongzhuang Road, Beijing, China

Distributed by China Publications Centre (Guoji Shudian)
P.O. Box 399, Beijing, China

Printed in the People's Republic of China

EDITOR'S NOTE

More than 30 years have elapsed since the birth of the People's Republic of China on October 1, 1949. "What is China really like today?" many people abroad wish to know. To answer this question, we plan to compile and publish a large-scale *China Handbook*, in which we shall introduce the New China in every field of its activities. Emphasis will be on the process of development during the past three decades, the accomplishments and the problems that still remain. The *Handbook* will contain accurate statistics and other material to serve as a reliable reference work as well as a comprehensive guide to New China.

To enhance the usefulness of the *Handbook*, we first plan to publish 10 major sections separately, so that we shall have an opportunity to take into consideration the opinions of our readers before the separate parts are put together, revised and published as one volume. These separate sections are:

Geography
History
Politics
Economy
Education and Science
Literature and the Arts
Sports and Public Health
Culture

Life and Lifestyles
Tourism

Readers are asked to note that (1) the statistics given in the separate volumes do not include Taiwan unless otherwise specified and (2) the statistics given in the separate volumes are valid as of the end of 1980.

CONTENTS

Chapter One
LITERATURE 1
1. Classical Literature (11th Century B.C.-A.D. 1840) 1
2. Modern Literature (1840-1919) 40
3. The Rise of Revolutionary Literature (1919-1949) 47
4. Contemporary Literature (1949-1981) 78

Chapter Two
THE ARTS 124
1. Theatre 124
2. The Cinema 144
3. Fine Arts 153
4. Handicrafts 169
5. Music 182
6. Dance 192
7. *Quyi* 204
8. Variety Arts: Acrobatics, Juggling, Conjuring and Circus Acts 209

Chapter One

LITERATURE

1. CLASSICAL LITERATURE (11th Century B.C.-A.D. 1840)

Classical Chinese literature is the literature produced in China during a period of over 3,000 years from the beginning of Chinese history to the Opium War. Its long history and splendid achievements are famous the world over. Its many great writers from all levels of the old society include Qu Yuan, Sima Qian, Tao Yuanming, Li Bai, Du Fu, Han Yu, Liu Zongyuan, Su Shi, Li Qingzhao, Xin Qiji, Guan Hanqing, Luo Guanzhong, Shi Naian, Pu Songling and Cao Xueqin. Masterpieces such as the *Book of Odes* and the "Li Sao", dating from pre-Qin times; Music Bureau ballads and *Records of the Historian*, dating from the Western Han; Tang and Song poetry and lyrics; Yuan drama and Ming and Qing fiction have all greatly enriched the treasure-house of Chinese literature.

(i) PRE-QIN LITERATURE (11TH CENTURY B.C.-221 B.C.)

Classical Chinese literature has its starting point during the course of the development of Chinese history from slave society to feudal society. The outstanding masterpieces from pre-Qin literature are the *Book of Odes*, dating from the Zhou Dynasty, the historical and philosophical prose of the Warring States and the "Li Sao" by Qu Yuan.

The *Book of Odes* The *Book of Odes* is the earliest collection of Chinese poetry, and consists of 305 poems written over a period of about 500 years during the Western Zhou and Spring and Autumn period. It was compiled in the 6th century B.C. and is divided into three parts. The first part, known as "Airs from the States", consists of 160 folk songs from 15 princely states under the Zhou; the "Greater Odes" and "Lesser Odes" make up the second part, consisting of 105 poems; and the "Eulogies", the third part, consists of 40 poems. The divisions are based on musical categories: regional music in the "Airs", music from the area directly under Zhou rule in the "Odes" and religious and ceremonial music in the "Eulogies". The poems in the *Book of Odes* are actually songs based on these musical types.

In terms of literary value, the folk songs in the "Airs" and "Lesser Odes" are particularly impressive. These oral compositions created by the working people touch on all aspects of current life and society, expressing protest at injustice and hope for love and happiness. "Seventh Month" (an air from Bin) describes the year-round arduous toil of the serfs and the oppression under which they suffered; "Cutting Wood" (an air from Wei) chastises the exploiters for enjoying the fruits of labour without working; and "Big Rats" (an air from Wei) expresses an even more bitter hatred of the exploiters. "The Broken Axe" and "The Eastern Mountain" (airs from Bin) show the sufferings caused by military campaigns and the people's desire to live in peace. Songs about love and marriage occupy a considerable portion of the *Book* of *Odes*, and most of them are sincere, natural and healthy. The folk songs in the *Book of Odes* indicate the working people's deep feelings towards life and their profound knowledge of it, in simple, beautiful language and fresh, vivid imagery, fully embodying the artistic creativeness of the people; they are the chief glory of the *Book of Odes*.

The *Book of Odes* is China's first work of realistic literature and as such has had a profound influence on the later development of poetry. Its abundant use of literary devices such as metaphor, allusion, repetition and antiphony has also been highly influential. All subsequent writers and poets of note in Chinese literary history have found it a rich source of inspiration.

Prose from the Warring States The Spring and Autumn and Warring States period is a period of transition from slave society to feudal society in China. At this time many different schools of thought flourished, a phenomenon known as the "contention between a hundred schools". The many different styles of historical and philosophical writing that appeared at this time laid the basis for the future development of Chinese prose.

In terms of literary value, the most important historical works of this period are the *Zuo Commentary* and the *Intrigues of the Warring States*. The most important philosophical works are the *Analects, Master Meng (Mencius), Master Mo, Master Xun, Master Zhuang, Master Han Fei* and *Lü's Spring and Autumn Annals,* and of these the *Analects, Master Meng* and *Master Zhuang* are especially notable for their high literary quality.

Qu Yuan and the "Li Sao" The first great poet known by name in Chinese literary history is Qu Yuan (340-278 B.C.), from the kingdom of Chu in the Warring

States period. A member of the Chu aristocracy, he was highly cultivated and nursed far-reaching political ambitions. As a young man he became the "Left Minister" of the state of Chu, ranking next to the prime minister and enjoying the king's confidence. Later, slanders against him led to his expulsion from court on the advice of traitorous ministers, and in despair he finally threw himself into a river and drowned. He left behind 25 poems, including "Li Sao", "The Odes", "The Elegies" and "The Riddles".[1] The "Li Sao" is his most well-known work. The title means something like affliction and sorrow. It is the longest lyrical poem in classical Chinese literature, consisting of 373 lines, and has a strong flavour of romanticism throughout. In deeply emotional and imaginative language the author expresses his patriotism, devotion to truth and hatred of evil. Breaking through the prosodic restriction of the *Book of Odes*, in which a four-character line predominates, the poet has created on the basis of Chu folk song the comparatively free "sao" style with lines of unequal length, thus adding greatly to the expressive power of the poem. The "Li Sao" and the *Book of Odes* are the two outstanding achievements in ancient Chinese poetry. Qu Yuan himself is a poet of world standing, and was one of the four cultural giants commemorated throughout the world in 1957.

(2) LITERATURE OF THE HAN (206 B.C.-A.D. 220)

The Qin Dynasty, which brought the independent kingdoms under one rule in a unified China, did not pro-

---

[1] English translation in *Li Sao and Other Poems of Qu Yuan*, Foreign Languages Press, Beijing, 1980.

duce any significant literary works itself, partly because it existed for only a brief period but partly also because of its policy of literary repression. Its successor, the Han Dynasty, brought in an age of economic and cultural expansion. Its most outstanding literary achievements are Sima Qian's *Records of the Historian*, the Music Bureau ballads and rhyme-prose compositions.

Sima Qian and *Records of the Historian* Sima Qian (c. 145-90 B.C.) is famous both as a writer and as a historian. He began to write his *Records of the Historian*[1] at the age of 42, completing it 11 years later. It covers a period of some 3,000 years, from the legendary age of the Yellow Emperor to Emperor Wu of the Han, in 130 sections and more than half a million words. It is the first comprehensive history in the form of biographical records in China. Many sections consist essentially of biographies of historical figures, and these emperors, kings, generals, ministers of state, assassins, warriors, actors, singing-girls and leaders of peasant uprisings come vividly to life as individual characters under the author's masterly pen. For this reason, the literary quality of this history has always been regarded as extremely high. As a model of biographical literature, *Records of the Historian* has had a strong influence on the literary development of later prose writing, including fiction and drama.

Music Bureau Ballads The Music Bureau was an administrative office established by Emperor Wu of the Han for the purpose of providing songs and music for state occasions, whose job included the collection of folk songs, in imitation of the Zhou Dynasty practice of folk

---

[1] Partial English translation in *Selections from Records of the Historian*, FLP, 1979.

song collection by state officials. The folk songs assembled by the Music Bureau from different areas, and later imitations in ballad form, were subsequently known collectively as Music Bureau ballads. It is believed that the number of folk songs collected at that time was quite considerable, but many have been lost and only 40 remain in existence, dating mostly from the Eastern Han. Music Bureau ballads generally have a five-character line and are cast as narratives. Most of them are oral compositions created by the masses at the lower levels of society, and hence give a broad and penetrating portrayal of life and society at that time. The narrative is lively, the characterization vivid and the imagery fresh and natural. Music Bureau narrative poetry reached a high peak under the Eastern Han, as represented by the anonymous "Flight of the Phoenix to the Southeast", which narrates the story of a minor official, Jiao Zhongqing, and his wife, Liu Lanzhi. They love each other deeply, but Jiao's cruel mother drives Liu back to her mother's home, where her brother forces her to marry the son of the local prefect. It ends with the young wife drowning herself on the eve of her second marriage, while Jiao hangs himself. In this domestic tragedy the author exposes the cruelty of feudal customs and evinces deep sympathy for the young couple who die in protest against convention. Skilfully constructed in a combination of narrative and lyrical elements, the poem is written in simple and vivid language and is a masterpiece of traditional realistic literature.

Han Rhyme-Prose Rhyme-prose is a form of composition combining elements of both poetry and prose, created by writers from the northern parts of the empire under the influence of Chu poetry from the south. It is divided into two categories, short pieces which are mostly lyrical, and longer pieces which are mostly elaborate descriptions of the splendours of royal gardens and cities. According to historical records, there were 1,000 rhyme-proses at the time of the Western Han. Early rhyme-prose writers include Jia Yi and Mei Cheng. Its peak period, from the time of Emperor Wu until the end of the Western Han, is represented by the most famous rhyme-prose writer, Sima Xiangru (179 B.C.-118 B.C.), in works such as "Master Void" and "Shanglin". The later period, in the early Eastern Han, is represented by Yang Xiong and Ban Gu. In the last years of the Eastern Han, several of the more creative writers, such as Zhang Heng, Zhao Yi, Cai Rong and Mi Heng, opposed the conventional and stereotyped style of Han rhyme-prose and created a new type that was more lyrical, shorter and with fewer allusions.

(3) LITERATURE OF WEI, JIN AND THE SOUTHERN AND NORTHERN DYNASTIES (220-581)

After peasant uprisings had destroyed the power of the Eastern Han Dynasty, a period of fighting followed in which three generals established virtually independent kingdoms, known by the dynastic names of Wei, Shu and Wu. Cao Cao, who occupied a large territory to the north, was the most powerful of these generals and also the most advanced politically and culturally. After his death in 220, his son Cao Pi became the first emperor of Wei. Many gifted writers assembled at the Wei capital and some excellent works were produced; the representative poets of this time include Cao Cao himself and his sons Cao Pi and Cao Zhi.

The Wei Dynasty was replaced by the Jin, which in 280 achieved a brief period of unity. Soon after, however, the country was divided into north and south, each ruled over by a succession of short-lived dynasties known in history as the Southern and Northern Dynasties. Writers reacted to the prevailing political turmoil and ruling class corruption by trying to escape from reality, and the depiction of life and society in their work is rather narrow. However, these conditions also produced some fine poets such as Tao Yuanming, who lived during the Eastern (Later) Jin Dynasty. The folk songs dating from the Southern and Northern Dynasties are also noteworthy and occupy a distinct position in Chinese literary history.

The period of Wei, Jin and the Southern and Northern Dynasties also saw a remarkable development in literary criticism in a struggle against the tendency towards formalism in literature.

Poets of the Cao Family and the Jian'an Period In the last years of the Eastern Han, the social order became very unsettled and war and rebellion were rife. A number of literary writers who were comparatively aware of reality and in sympathy with the people wrote poems in imitation of the Music Bureau ballads, depicting the war-torn society around them and the people's sufferings, and voicing their hopes for reunification. The literature of this period is known as Jian'an literature, after the last effective reign period of the Han Dynasty, from 196 to 220. Cao Cao and his sons Cao Pi and Cao Zhi are the best-known poets of Jian'an literature. Cao Cao (155-220), the famous general and strategist who founded the Wei Dynasty, was also a noted poet. Two short songs attributed to him, "The Burial Ground" and "Dew on the Shallots", depict the unsettled conditions at the end of Han. He is best known for his "Short Songs", which express his ambition to found a new dynasty and surround himself with men of ability. His "Gazing at the Ocean" is a masterpiece of descriptive writing. His great strength of will and resolution are given full play in his strong and vigorous poetry. Cao Pi (187-226), his eldest son and first emperor of Wei, is known chiefly for his five-character line poems about love and separation. His "Song of Yan" is the earliest example of a seven-character line poem. In terms of artistic achievement, however, both father and eldest son are overshadowed by Cao Zhi (192-232), whose most well-known works include "The White Horse" and "Presented to Biao, King of Baima". The personal sincerity of Cao Zhi's poems is matched by the fresh and lively grace of his style. He paid great attention to matters of artistic form and has always been greatly admired for the beauty of his sentiments and their expression.

The "Seven Jian'an Masters" — Kong Rong (153-208), Wang Can (177-217), Liu Zhen (?-217), Ruan Yu (c. 165-212), Xu Gan (171-218), Chen Lin (?-217), Ying Chang (?-217) — are also noted poets, and except for Kong Rong, were all part of a literary coterie at the Cao court during the Jian'an period.

Tao Yuanming After the fall of the Han, Confucian ideology was undermined and replaced by the new religion Buddhism. Taoist nihilism, based on the teachings of Master Lao and Master Zhuang, also flourished for a while, and metaphysical discussion became a popular pastime among men of learning. In literature this tendency led to poetry about mysticism and the search for immortality, while preoccupation with form also became widespread. The Jin poet Tao Yuanming, towering above his contemporaries, was the sole figure to defy this counter-current in literature.

Tao Yuanming (365-427) was born into a landlord family in decline. He once held a minor official appointment, but his upright nature led him to despise the corrupt life of the bureaucracy, and he left office to return to the countryside to live as a recluse. Most of the 120 poems that survive describe rural scenery and his life in retirement. Among his most famous poems are a set of five verses under the title "Returning to Live in the Country", which express his new emotions after leaving office and describe the life of toil and the natural scenery around his home. Poems such as "Drinking Wine", "Miscellaneous Poems" and "Song to Jing Ke" also express his ideals, his aims in life and his indignation and distress at being unable to achieve his ambitions. Tao Yuanming is also noted for his essays and rhyme-prose, such as "A Record of the Peach Blossom Spring", "Biography of the Gentleman of the Five Willows" and "The Return". Both in poetry and prose the language he uses is natural and unadorned, and his style is simple and fresh with no trace of the ornamentation common at that time. Although in his own lifetime his poetry was not highly thought of, his influence on later poets was considerable.

Folk Songs of the Southern and Northern Dynasties The folk songs of the 5th and 6th centuries followed in the tradition of the Music Bureau ballads but were shorter in length and lyrical rather than narrative. Because of political, economic and cultural differences between north and south, the folk songs from different areas have different characteristics. The southern folk songs have a comparatively narrow thematic range that concentrates mostly on the joys and sorrows of love and separation, giving voice to the complex emotions of women in feudal society who are oppressed but powerless to resist. These poems are delicate and polished. In the north, because of continual warfare and the intermingling of different ethnic groups, the folk songs give a broader picture of life and society, and a considerable number are specifically concerned with unjust wars and the people's sufferings. These poems are bold, robust and resolute. "The Ballad of Mulan" is an outstanding example, comparable to "Flight of the Phoenix to the Southeast". It tells the story of a young girl called Mulan who equips herself as a soldier to go to war in her father's place, and her heroic spirit informs the whole poem. It has been a popular favourite for centuries and is known by heart in many village families.

Fiction of Wei, Jin and the Southern and Northern Dynasties The popularity of fiction relating tales of the supernatural and scholars' anecdotes dates from this period. *Records of Spirits* by Gan Bao of the Eastern Jin Dynasty is a typical collection of supernatural fiction, and *New Anecdotes of Social Talk* by Liu Yiqing of the Southern Dynasties' Song is a typical collection of anecdotal fiction. Both types of stories are constructed as short tales. In written form they retain a great deal of feudal superstition, but they also preserve many excellent folk tales and thoughtful anecdotes, and had a considerable influence on the later development of anecdotal fiction.

Literary Criticism The development of creative literature in the period of Wei, Jin and the Southern and Northern Dynasties was accompanied by the appearance of works on literary criticism, which drew both on the experiences of earlier writers and the author's own impressions. The most notable of these efforts are:

1. "Essay on Literature" by Cao Pi, the oldest work devoted to literary criticism that has survived. It affirms the value of literature and is the first attempt at an exposition on style.

2. "Rhyme-Prose on Literature" by Lu Ji (261-303), which discusses a series of questions concerning literature, such as the relationship between form and content, the special characteristics of literary genres, style and structure.

3. *Intent and Ornament in Literature* by Liu Xie (c. 466-c. 520), which consists altogether of 50 sections arranged in 10 parts. It expounds the origins of literature and its special characteristics, notes the experience of earlier writers and proposes methods and standards in literary criticism. It is the first systematic work on literary theory in Chinese literary history.

4. *The Classification of Poets* by Zhong Rong (?-552), a systematic evaluation of over 100 poets and their work from the Han Dynasty to the Southern Liang. The author urges a more vigorous kind of poetry than was then current and criticizes metaphysical poetry. Works like *Intent and Ornament in Literature* and *The Classification of Poets* strongly attacked the formalism then prevalent in literature.

(4) TANG LITERATURE (618-907)

The Tang Dynasty was a period of great economic prosperity and cultural growth in Chinese feudal society. Among the factors promoting the development of Tang literature are political and social stability, the system of selecting officials according to literary ability, and contacts between Chinese and foreign cultures. Tang literature is most famous for its poetry, which reaches new heights of romanticism and realism; the Tang is known as the golden age of Chinese classical poetry. *The Complete Tang Poetry* in its present version contains almost 50,000 poems by more than 2,200 poets, including poets of world stature such as Li Bai, Du Fu and Bai Juyi. A movement for reform in literary prose writing, led by Han Yu and Liu Zongyuan, also took place during Tang, and a number of outstanding essays were produced which were taken as models by later generations of essayists. Further, a type of prose romance whose beginnings accompanied the growth of cities in China opened up a path for the later development of short story writing.

Tang Poetry The development of Tang poetry is usually divided into three stages, early, high and late. In early Tang poetry, the formalism and ornamentation of 5th and 6th century poetry still prevailed. A new atmosphere was created with the poetry of Wang Bo (648-676), Yang Jiong (650-?), Lu Zhaolin (c. 635-c. 689) and Luo Binwang (c. 640-?), who broke through the narrow confines of poetry about court life and wrote in a fresh and lively style, giving poetry a new vitality. A more conscious attempt at reform was later initiated by Chen Ziang (661-702), who eliminated the remaining vestiges of formalism in his work. His concern with current social problems is reflected in poems which express his individual political aims and his frustration at being overlooked. His poetry is robust, simple and resolute, and his reforms paved the way for the subsequent development of Tang poetry to its highest peak.

Chinese poetry entered the stage of its highest achievements during the reign of Emperor Xuanzong (r. 712-756; also known as Minghuang); this is the high Tang period. Two important forms of poetry came to maturity at this time: "regulated" poetry, an eight line verse form with either five or seven characters per line, and strictly regulated in regard to tone patterns, choice of words and so on; and "cut-short" poetry, a four line version of the regulated form where the central idea is implied rather than openly stated. The earlier, unregulated poetry with five or seven characters a line continued to be popular but was henceforth known as "old-style" poetry. More than a thousand poets appeared at this time and their poems can be counted by the tens of thousands. Many different styles and schools emerged in this remarkable profusion of literary talent.

Landscape poetry is represented by Meng Haoran and Wang Wei. The extant work of Meng Haoran (689-740) includes some 260 poems. Using a very strict five-character line and skilful rhyming, he wrote a great number of landscape and pastoral poems, depicting high mountains and great rivers, the dwellings of hermits hidden deep in the forests, and the pleasures and sorrows of high officials. Sentiment and nature are blended in his poetry with a high degree of skill. The extant work of Wang Wei (701-761) includes more than 400 poems. Most of his works describe his secluded life and natural scenery. Because of his great talents in painting, calligraphy and music, his poetry is specially characterized by brilliant colour and fresh imagery. It is commonly said of him that there is poetry in his painting and painting in his poetry.

Frontier poetry is represented by Gao Shi, Cen Shen and Wang Changling. The poetry of Gao Shi (702-765) and Cen Shen (716-770) describes the ever-changing border scenery and the generals and soldiers at the frontier defences galloping across the wastelands, and is charged with the heroic spirit of those who resist the enemy in defence of their country. Their poems also depict the sufferings of conscripts and soldiers in military campaigns, and show the conflicts between various ethnic groups, officers and soldiers, and rulers and ruled. Among the frontier poets, Wang Changling (698-757) is particularly skilful at conveying the thoughts and emotions of the soldiers serving at the frontiers.

The twin peaks of high Tang poetry are the romantic poetry of Li Bai and the realistic poetry of Du Fu. The greatest poets of the Tang, Li Bai and Du Fu are also the outstanding representatives of realism and romanticism in classical Chinese poetry.

Li Bai (701-762) is the first great romantic poet after Qu Yuan, and like Qu Yuan his life included exile from court and long periods of wandering. Because he looked with contempt on the powerful families at court and passionately defended his freedom, he repeatedly came under their attack. He died in 762, destitute and homeless.

Li Bai's extant work includes more than 900 poems. They cover a broad thematic range and touch on all aspects of life and society. There are songs in praise of resistance to autocracy and support for acts of chivalry, and also poems exposing ruling class corruption and the darker aspects of society, such as "Song of the Gallant Swordsman", "Ancient Poems" (59 poems) and "Hard Is the Way". Although some of his poems written during the years of frustration and adversity reflect his loneliness, pessimism and escapism, nevertheless most are strongly positive, full of contempt for autocracy, dissatisfaction with reality and a yearning for freedom, such as "Bring in the Wine" and "Farewell Song to the Queen of the Sky, After a Dream Journey". Travelling widely across famous mountains and great rivers in his lifetime, Li Bai wrote a large quantity of poems in which depiction of natural beauty is combined with narrative and lyricism, such as "An Early Start from White Emperor City", "Gazing at Lushan Waterfall" and "Steep Is the Way to Shu". His genius for description is equally well employed in the depiction of delicate beauty and imposing grandeur, and many of these lines have been constantly quoted through the ages. Many of his works also describe a woman's true love and sorrow at parting, and his songs in praise of friendship are particularly noteworthy. In developing his own artistic style, Li Bai drew on the tradition of romanticism inherited from Qu Yuan, adopting the techniques of exaggeration and condensation from folk songs and employing legend and his own imagination to express his daring and passion. His language is extremely beautiful and natural, with many variations in the use of tones and harmony. His influence on the development of Tang and later poetry is considerable.

Du Fu (712-770) lived at the turning point of the Tang Dynasty when its prosperity began to decline. The immediate cause was the rebellion led by An Lushan and Shi Siming, which lasted from 756 to 763 and forced the Tang court into exile. Although he was a member of the scholar class, Du Fu lived through the disasters of the period alongside the common people. In an attempt to flee the rebels, he was captured and forced to remain in the occupied capital. He finally managed to escape and join the exiled court, where already middle-aged, he was appointed a low-ranking counsellor, his first official post. His blunt memorials led to his dismissal, and together with his family he moved several times before settling down in Chengdu. He died while travelling again in Hunan, leaving to posterity over 1,400 poems.[1]

The unsettled times in which he lived and his own personal misfortunes brought Du Fu close to the people at the lower levels of society, and his poems reach a depth never before achieved in classical Chinese poetry. Many are relentless exposures of ruling class society, and his indictments were levelled directly at its highest ranking members, as in "Ballad of Beautiful Ladies", and "Washing Weapons". Another group expresses his strong admiration for the hard work and courage of the common people; this includes "Song of the Firewood Vendors" and "Song of the Ablest Men". Of particular importance are the poems in which he describes the terrible sufferings inflicted on the people by the fighting and disturbances, such as "Going Out of the Frontier" and "Ballad of the War Chariots", and especially the "Three Officers" and "Three Partings" sets of poems. "The Shihao Officer", one of the "Three Officers" poems, relates in a particularly trenchant and moving way an example of the hardship experienced by the people in times of civil disturbance and foreign invasion. Throughout his life Du Fu was deeply concerned with politics, and many of his poems are on current events. His landscape and pastoral poems are also very highly regarded.

---

[1] A selection of Du Fu's poems in English translation is given in *Tu Fu: Selected Poems*, FLP, 1964.

Du Fu inherited the realistic tradition in literature which stems from the *Book of Odes*. His approach is objective and serious and his tone is profound and solemn, touched with melancholy and resolution. His language is concise, trenchant and powerful, and he excels in introducing popular expressions into his verse. He is also extremely skilful in employing rhyme, tone variation and metre, so that his poems are even better read aloud and their emotional expressiveness is greatly enhanced. He is regarded as a model by all later poets — no writer in the history of Chinese literature has had as broad a following as Du Fu.

In the latter half of the high Tang period, from 742 to 779, several other poets such as Liu Changqing, Wei Yingwu and Li Yi were relatively enlightened politically and sympathetic towards the people, and had some influence on the further development of poetry.

The late Tang period, from 780 to the end of the dynasty in 907, saw the gradual disintegration of central imperial authority. At court, power passed into the hands of the eunuchs as the ruling elite became increasingly corrupt. Under these circumstances, many poets believed that Music Bureau style ballads would be able to depict the people's sufferings, and for a time new ballads in this style flourished. Among the famous balladeers of the time were Zhang Ji, Wang Jian and Yuan Zhen, but the most outstanding was Bai Juyi.

Bai Juyi grew up in poverty but was able to enter the civil service and served for a time as imperial counsellor. However, he was relegated to a minor post after submitting repeated memorials to the throne criticizing current abuses. He later served as governor and minister. Towards the end of his life he settled in Luoyang, at some distance from the capital, where he lived in seclusion. He divided his poetry into four parts: satirical, occasional, sentimental and miscellaneous. The satirical poems, which number over 170, are the richest in realistic significance. Some expose the corruption and cruelty of the ruling elite and attack the extortionate taxes levelled by the state, such as "The Old Charcoal Seller", "The Old Man with the Broken Arm" and "The Captive". Others are protests at injustices in women's lives, such as "A Mother's Farewell to Her Son" and "The White-Haired Woman". Bai Juyi is particularly noted for his long narrative poems, "Song of Everlasting Remorse" and "Lute Song", which both enjoyed an extremely wide circulation. The former relates a popular legend about the late emperor Minghuang and his concubine Lady Yang, adding many details out of his imagination for greater artistic effect and written in fluent and natural language. The latter uses the unhappy life of a former lute-girl, now abandoned by her admirers, to express his own indignation at injustice in a very sad and moving poem. Bai Juyi also left behind 1,914 regulated poems of which more than 700 are in cut-short form. His poems are fresh, moving and easy to read, standard-bearers for the current school of "popular poetry". In the poet's own lifetime they won widespread admiration and popularity. They were greatly prized in Japan and Korea and are known throughout the world today.

Yuan Zhen's name is often linked with Bai Juyi. Early in his career, Yuan Zhen (779-831) came to share Bai Juyi's views on literature and was a strong supporter of the new Music Bureau ballad. However, his poetry falls below his friend's in depth of realism and mastery of the vernacular.

Among other famous poets of late Tang are Li He, Liu Yuxi, Jia Dao, Meng Jiao, Li Shangyin, Wen Tingyun and Du Mu. These poets were chiefly concerned with creating original artistic effects and made contributions of varying importance in the development of form in poetry.

The Revival of Classical Prose The period of the Southern and Northern Dynasties saw a tendency towards excessive ornamentation in prose. Known as "parallel prose", this style was characterized by regulations on tones, parallelism and antithesis, and the piling up of allusions to earlier literature, history and legend. Its emphasis on form to the neglect of content was a serious obstacle in the further development of prose writing. Two famous poets and essayists, Han Yu and Liu Zongyuan, led the attack on parallel prose, encouraging the revival of the classical style of pre-Qin prose and demanding equal emphasis on substance. In what amounted to a great liberation in writing, they replaced parallel prose with a much looser form of prose and developed a style that was both lucid and vigorous. The essay as an independent literary genre, quite apart from historical and philosophical writing, dates from this time.

Han Yu (768-824) is most admired for his concise and vigorous essays on miscellaneous topics. His discursive essays, such as "On the Origin of the Way", "On the Origin of Destruction" and "A Talk on Instruction", have also won great respect from writers throughout the ages. In a few hundred words, the author delivers a penetrating exposition which is emphatic, vivid and logical. His funeral addresses, prefaces and biographical sketches are also fine examples of prose writing. Han Yu is famous as a master of language with great powers of exposition and many of the expressions in his writing have become set phrases widely used in the Chinese language.

Liu Zongyuan (773-819) wrote many different kinds of essays, his most original being satirical fables and travel essays. He developed the anecdotes or fables found in the writings of pre-Qin philosophers into short literary essays complete in themselves, thus establishing the fable as an independent literary form. He injected into his fables a strong note of realism, transforming them into militant and satirical compositions.[1] The famous "Three Cautions", for instance, about deer, donkeys and rats respectively, are satires on people who forget all restraint once they have achieved their desires, taking advantage of their favoured position and caring only for self-aggrandizement. Liu Zongyuan also excelled at depicting natural scenery, his most representative work being "Eight Sketches of Yongzhou". In a new departure for travel essays, his descriptions of scenery are pervaded with a sense of his own suffering and melancholy. His biographical sketches are also an important part of his work: "Song Qing", "Camel-Back Guo", "The Nurseryman" and "The Carpenter" describe the noble qualities and skilled craft of traders in medicinal herbs, carpenters and gardeners, people at the lowest levels of society. Another famous essay, "The Snake Catchers", which relates the story of the Jiang family who for three generations preferred to risk death through snakebite than perish under harsh governmental taxes, exposes the ruthless oppression of the exploiting class. Both in ideological content and artistic skill, Liu Zongyuan is superior to Han Yu as an essayist.

---

[1] Some of these fables are included in *Chinese Ancient Fables*, FLP, 1981.

Tang Prose Romances Before the Tang Dynasty, fiction writing was still in its infancy. Among the factors which promoted its growth in the Tang were the development of commerce, increasing urban prosperity and the city dwellers' need for cultural amusements. The short tales written in the literary language which appeared at this time are known as "prose romances". Among the more famous romances are "The Story of the Pillow", which ridicules infatuation with fame and office, and "The Story of Li Wa" (also known as "The Story of a Singsong Girl"), "The Story of Liu Yi" (also known as "The Dragon King's Daughter") and the "The Story of Huo Xiaoyu" (also known as "Prince Huo's Daughter"), all stories about love.[1] Tang prose romances were to provide a source of material for fiction writers and dramatists in the Yuan, Ming and Qing.

(5) LITERATURE OF THE SONG AND YUAN DYNASTIES (960-1368)

The fall of the Tang Dynasty was followed by more than fifty years of division before the country was finally reunited under the Song. In the period of Song rule, from the Northern Song (960-1127) which ruled over the whole country to the Southern Song (1127-1280) which only ruled the area south of the Changjiang (Yangtze River), the extravagance and indulgence of the ruling class encouraged a tendency towards an extravagant and dissolute aestheticism. Some of the progressive intellectuals of the time were unhappy about this trend, and

---

[1] Ten of these stories are included in *The Dragon King's Daughter*, FLP. 1980.

reforms in poetry and prose were carried out in a movement led by Ouyang Xiu and backed by Wang Anshi and Su Shi. The call for simple and plain writing won wide support, and Song poetry and prose were brought back on the path of healthy development. Su Shi subsequently extended the reform in poetry and prose to the new lyric form. As the lyric was broadened and deepened by involvement in the real world, it reached its peak of perfection at this time in the hands of poets such as Su Shi, Xin Qiji and Li Qingzhao, and many outstanding works were created.

With the development of commerce and handicrafts under the Song and the increasing prosperity of the cities, city dwellers as a group also grew stronger, and a literature and art came into being that depicted urban life and suited urban tastes. The art of storytelling and the appearance of prompt-books for the use of storytellers created new literary forms which laid the basis for the subsequent development of vernacular fiction and drama.

In 1279, the Yuan Dynasty conquered the Southern Song and reunited China. The outstanding achievements of the Yuan Dynasty in literature are the dramatic lyric and Yuan drama. Within a period of less than 90 years, a large number of dramatists made their appearance, headed by Guan Hanqing, and many excellent works were produced. Traditional drama reached its peak at this time.

Song Dynasty Lyrics The Chinese lyric is a type of poetry with lines of unequal length and set to music. Its origins go back to the Southern Dynasties of the 5th and 6th centuries, but as an independent poetic form it is a product of the late Tang. Nevertheless, it was still closely related to song, and the individual pieces are still known primarily by the name of the tune to which they are set, which determines the strict pattern of tones, rhymes and line structure; it is not generally classed as poetry proper in China. The lyric reached its full development under the Song and is a major achievement of Song literature.

Song Dynasty lyrics may be divided into two groups, one known for its grace and the other for its vigour. Representative poets of the former type include Liu Yong, Qin Guan, Zhou Bangyan and Li Qingzhao. Their lyrics are mostly confined to two themes, love and sorrow at parting, and are written in a tender and graceful style. Li Qingzhao (1084-1151) is the most outstanding poet of this school, though only 50 of her lyrics have survived. Although she mostly writes of love and sorrow, there is no sign of weakness in her deeply felt lyrics. She was especially skilful at creating fresh new imagery and a beautiful, highly polished language. Lyrics such as "To the tune of 'Reddening the Lips' ", on a lively young woman, "To the tune of 'Drunk Under Flower Shadows' ", on grief in love, and "To the tune 'Spring in Wuling' " and "To the tune 'Each Sound Slowly' ", on personal misfortune at a time of national calamity and the sorrow of losing home and kindred, have been recognized by generations as works of the highest literary quality.

The vigorous type of lyric is represented in the works of Su Shi of the Northern Song and Xin Qiji of the Southern Song. Su Shi (1037-1101), his father Su Xun and his brother Su Che were all famous writers. Su Shi (also known as Su Dongbo) was remarkably accomplished in many different literary genres, but his position in the development of the lyric is particularly important. He broadened its range and elevated its literary status by introducing themes such as the description of natural scenery and historical sites. The range of his own lyrics is very broad. "Hunting at Mizhou — To the tune 'River City'" portrays the author's emotions as he goes on a tiger hunt and his wish to defend his country against invasion; "When Will the Bright Moon Come? — To the tune of 'Waterside Song'" portrays the frustration of unemployed talent and unfulfilled ambition; "Remembering the Past at Red Cliff — To the tune 'Remembering Her Charm'" describes the scenic beauty and heroic past of the poet's homeland in bold, sweeping strokes.

In 1127, the Nüzhen (Jurchen or "Golden Tartars") drove the Song Dynasty from north China and established their own dynasty, the Kin Dynasty. The loss of territory affected the development of the lyric, and many Southern Song lyrics express fervent patriotism and resolution. Xin Qiji (1140-1207) is the outstanding example of the patriotic lyricists of this time. During his youth he fought against the Nüzhen and all his life urged resistance to the Kin. However, none of the proposals he made for the recovery of lost territory were accepted, and instead he himself came under attack by the rulers and various factions at court. For long periods he was out of office and living in retirement. The 600 lyrics he has left behind express his longing for the recovery of national unity, his frustration at not being able to realize his ambitions and his criticism of the capitulationist acts of the Southern Song ruling elite, in a bold and resolute style. His landscape lyrics are also known for their fresh, romantic charm. Among his best-known works are: "A Lyric Expressing Resolution Sent to Chen Tongfu — To the tune of 'Dance of the Cavalry'" and "Mounting the

Mind-Pleasing Pavilion at Jiankang — To the tune of 'Water Dragon's Chant' ".

Poetry and Prose A large number of famous writers appeared during and after the reform movement in Song poetry and prose. Among them are the Northern Song writers Ouyang Xiu, Wang Anshi, Su Shi, Su Xun, Su Che and Zeng Gong, who are often linked with the late Tang writers Han Yu and Liu Zongyuan as the "Eight Great Writers of Tang and Song". The Southern Song is represented by Lu You.

Ouyang Xiu (1007-1072) was a many-sided writer whose notable achievements include poetry, lyrics, essays — discursive, narrative, travel and literary — and history. His prose style is graceful and lively.

Wang Anshi (1021-1086), at one time prime minister, was a famous political reformer and thinker. His fame as one of the "Eight Great Writers" rests on his political essays, but his poetry is actually superior, especially his realistic poems on historical and current events.

Su Shi completed the reform in poetry and prose with his free, natural style. His many essays on pavilions and terraces are characterized by the combination of description, narrative and criticism, and his more than 4,000 surviving poems depict an even broader range of social life than his lyrics and essays.

Lu You (1125-1210) was a famous patriotic poet of the Southern Song who strenuously advocated opposition to the Kin throughout his life. Although he was elbowed aside and attacked by the capitulationists, his patriotic faith never wavered. One of the most prolific poets in Chinese literary history, he left behind more than 9,300 poems. The most outstanding characteristic of his poetry is the expression of his ardent patriotism. His heroic and resolute spirit is represented in "Expressing Indignation" and "Night Mooring at a River Village". Poems like "Moon over the Mountain Pass", "Going Beyond the Frontier", "Indignation" and "Drunken Song" express his indignation at the Southern Song's policy of non-resistance, and "Peasant Lament", "Autumn Harvest" and "Autumn Thoughts" reflect the popular distress and the hopes of the people in the occupied areas. Lu You excelled in several verse forms, including old-style, regulated, cut-short and lyrics. His seven-character line regulated verse is particularly outstanding and is rated by some as on the same level as Du Fu's. His lyrics, of which over 100 survive, are light and graceful, but many are also filled with patriotic fervour. His poems and lyrics bring a note of rousing militancy to Song poetry.

Song Storytellers' Scripts The development in China of short stories written in the vernacular is closely related to the art of storytelling, a form of folk literature that developed along with the growth of cities. Professional storytellers gathered in the market-places to tell their tales, and some of these stories were transcribed to act as prompt books for the storyteller. During the Song these storytellers' scripts or prompt books were compiled by people outside the profession, and new stories were written in the same style; these stories are also referred to as storytellers' scripts to indicate their origin.

Storytellers' scripts fall into three main categories: "small talk" (i.e. fiction), tales from history and tales from the Buddhist scriptures, the most notable being the purely fictional tales. According to records, 115 Song storytellers' scripts are known to have existed, but only 20-30 have survived. Among the most famous of the fiction scripts are "The Jade Worker" and "Fifteen Strings of Cash".[1] The stories generally describe life among the lower classes of urban society, reflecting popular ideas and attacking feudal morality, and feature complex plots and realistic narrative. Beginnings are made in the portrayal of characters as individuals, such as townswomen who boldly seek love and freedom, rapacious landlords, despotic officials and clever and upright heroes. The stories employ a popular language which is lively, simple and witty, and townspeople make their first appearance in literature, thus greatly enlarging its scope. The use of the vernacular in creative writing opened a new path in the development of language in literature, and gave literature a broader mass basis.

Yuan Vari-Drama and Free-Song The most notable achievement of Yuan literature is vari-drama, which emerged around the end of the Kin and the beginning of Yuan. It consists basically of a single and complete story in four acts or song sequences, and has the unique characteristic that the songs or arias are sung only by the protagonist, either male or female. Apart from the arias, there are also dialogue, stage action and dance, performed to musical accompaniment. This comprehensive dramatic form was created jointly by actors, musicians and playwrights on the basis of northern folk drama, and touches on all levels of Yuan society. Regarded in its own time as merely popular entertainment, it received little attention from literary scholars and not much is known about the lives of even its most famous creators, such as Guan

---

[1] English translation of both stories published in *The Courtesan's Jewel Box*, FLP, 1981.

Hanqing, Wang Shifu, Ma Zhiyuan and Bai Pu. Nevertheless 530 Yuan vari-dramas have survived, including masterpieces such as *Snow in Midsummer* (also known as *The Wrongs of Dou E*), *The Western Chamber* and *The Orphan of Zhao*, whose appeal after several hundred years is still fresh both in China and abroad.

Guan Hanqing (c. 1213-c. 1297) wrote 67 plays of which 18 survive (including five in incomplete form). They include *Snow in Midsummer, Rescued by a Coquette, The Jade Mirror-Stand, The Wife-Snatcher* and *Lord Guan Goes to the Feast*.[1] *Snow in Midsummer*, a tragedy about a virtuous young woman from an ordinary home who is punished for a crime she did not commit, is his best-known work. Her defiant spirit, in Guan Hanqing's representation, had the power to move heaven and earth to redress her wrongs. The play has been regarded as a classic of Chinese tragedy. Guan Hanqing's works also include comedy, courtroom drama and historical drama. His characters are rich and varied, creatures of flesh and blood, and he is skilled at presenting character and reflecting social contradictions through dramatic conflict. His language is also fresh and lively. A dramatist who made outstanding contributions to literary history, Guan Hanqing was one of the giants of world culture commemorated throughout the world in 1958.

Wang Shifu (fl. late 13th, early 14th centuries) wrote 14 plays, of which only three survive in complete form. *The Western Chamber* is his most successful work, and the best of Yuan romantic drama. Through the story of a beautiful girl, Cui Yingying, and a talented young

---

[1] English translations of these plays have been published under the title *Selected Plays of Guan Hanqing*, FLP, 1979.

scholar, Zhang, whose love defies feudal conventions, it satirizes feudal ethics and praises the lovers' victorious struggle for freedom of choice in marriage.

Bai Pu (1226-1306) wrote 16 plays, mostly on the theme of love, of which only two remain. His most famous work is *Rain on the Plantain Tree*, about the ill-fated love between the Tang emperor Minghuang and his concubine Lady Yang.

Ma Zhiyuan (c. 1250-1324) wrote 13 plays, of which seven survive. His most famous work is *Autumn in the Han Palace*, about the Emperor Yuan of Han and the palace maid Wang Jiang.

Ji Junxiang (fl. late 13th century) is known mainly for his *The Orphan of Zhao*, one of the first Chinese plays to be translated into a European language.

Yuan free-song was a new form of rhymed verse which developed out of northern popular ballads and folk songs. The tunes on which its versification are based are derived from several different ethnic groups and do not correspond to Song lyric tunes. Most free-songs are quite short, consisting of only one stanza and known as *xiaoling*, or minor songs, but there are also longer ones consisting of two or more stanzas and known as *taoqu*, or free-song sets. The names of 187 Yuan free-song writers have been recorded, many of them also writers of vari-drama such as Guan Hanqing, Bai Pu and Ma Zhiyuan. Ma Zhiyuan was the most important of the early Yuan free-song writers, and 120 of his free-songs have been preserved, mostly laments about the times, descriptions of nature and love songs. The later Yuan free-song writers gradually lost the characteristic simplicity and naturalness of their predecessors, and their work became increasingly flowery and superficial.

(6) LITERATURE FROM THE MING TO THE LATE QING DYNASTY (1368-1840)

The Ming and Qing dynasties saw the decline of feudalism in China. Handicraft industries advanced and the beginnings of a capitalist economy were emerging. Political power became concentrated to an unprecedented degree in the hands of the emperor, and class contradictions became increasingly acute. The Manchu Qing Dynasty practised racial discrimination, and contradictions between ethnic groups also became acute. The spread of democratic and nationalist ideas gave the progressive literature of this period its characteristic anti-feudal flavour. The traditional episodic novel made great progress in works like *Romance of the Three Kingdoms, Outlaws of the Marsh, Journey to the West, A Dream of Red Mansions* and *The Scholars*. The Qing collection of short fiction in the literary language, *Strange Tales of Liaozhai*, was also a notable achievement, and works such as *The Peony Pavilion, The Palace of Eternal Youth* and *Peach Blossom Fan* were masterpieces of dramatic writing.

The Episodic Novel The traditional Chinese novel as developed during the Ming and Qing is episodic in nature, relating the adventures of a large number of characters in a string of loosely connected events. Its thematic range is broad, including historical romances, chivalric tales, ghost stories, social satire and love stories. The early Ming novel was mostly produced on the basis of Song and Yuan historical tales and storytellers' scripts, compiled and polished by one or more authors, as in *Romance of the Three Kingdoms, Outlaws of the Marsh* and *Journey to the West*. The novel as the creation of an individual writer, such as *Jin Ping Mei*, began to appear around the middle of the Ming. The latter development reached its peak under the Qing, in novels like *A Dream of Red Mansions* and *The Scholars*.

The *Romance of the Three Kingdoms* is a historical romance set in the last years of the Eastern Han and the Three Kingdoms period, tracing the rise and fall of the three kingdoms of Wei, Shu and Wu. The present text is thought to have been compiled by Luo Guanzhong on the basis of existing written and oral accounts of the Three Kingdoms period. The novel vividly depicts the turbulent social conditions at that time, as the rulers of the three independent kingdoms struggled for supremacy. Its panoramic scope includes a cast of over 400 characters, and its central figures, Cao Cao, Liu Bei, Zhuge Liang, Guan Yu and Zhang Fei have captured the imaginations of generations of readers. The author also excels in battle scenes, no two of the many battle scenes being depicted alike. The language, a mixture of the literary and the vernacular, is easy and fluent. Its appearance gave rise to many other historical novels and plays about the Three Kingdoms, and in the repertoire of 19th-century Beijing Opera there were more than 100 such works.

Outlaws of the Marsh[1] (also known as *Water Margin* and *All Men Are Brothers*) is the first novel in China about peasant uprisings in feudal society. Its authorship is uncertain but has been attributed to Shi Naian (early Ming) and Luo Guanzhong. The author or authors collected material from oral legends, storytellers' scripts and vari-drama, providing continuity between unconnected episodes and improving the literary quality. The book

---

[1] English translation published by FLP, 1980.

relates the stories of the 108 men and women who gathered at Liangshan (in present Shandong) under the leadership of Song Jiang during the Northern Song, and shows the inevitable process of peasant revolts from their initial occurrence through to defeat, reflecting basic contradictions in Chinese feudal society. The novel represents a new advance in the art of fiction in the delineation of character growth and development, showing the heroes' reactions to their changes in fortune in terms of their origins and experiences. The language of *Outlaws* is a refinement of northern colloquial speech and is fresh, lively and humorous. *Outlaws of the Marsh* became not only a source for many later literary works but also a powerful weapon in the resistance of the popular masses in feudal society.

Journey to the West[1] (also known as *Pilgrimage to the West* and *Monkey*) is a mythological novel dating from mid-Ming. Although the episodic nature of the traditional novel continued well into the Qing, by mid-Ming the role of the author had already become more important in the creation and arrangement of material. Wu Cheng'en (c. 1500-1582) based his version of *Journey to the West* on existing popular legends and written tales, but his imaginative use of the material and his skill in organizing the vast scale of this work are major contributions. The main part of *Journey* is a series of episodes relating the adventures of the Tang Dynasty monk Xuanzang (commonly referred to as Tripitaka) on a pilgrimage to the Western Regions (i.e. India) in search of Buddhist scriptures. He is accompanied by several mythological figures led by the real hero of the novel, Sun Wukong (Monkey).

---

[1] English translation of volume one published by FLP, 1982; volumes two and three forthcoming.

The adventures of Sun Wukong and the others, related in a fluent, lively style, constitute China's most famous comic masterpiece. After it came many other novels of the supernatural but even the best of these, *The Canonization of the Gods*, is much inferior to *Journey to the West*.

The Scholars[1] (also known as *The Informal History of the Literati*) by Wu Jingzi (1701-1754) is a satirical novel about the destructive effects of the examination system on men of talent and the despicable nature of the class of bureaucrats it creates. It also exposes the avarice of the bureaucrat landlords and the hypocrisy of feudal ethics. Modelling his work on earlier satirical literature, the author selected incidents from real life and reworked them to make them more typical, sketching them in cartoon-like images in a simple, lively style. *The Scholars* laid the foundation for the later Chinese satirical novel and was an important influence on the late Qing novels of denunciation.

A Dream of Red Mansions[2] (also known as *Dream of the Red Chamber* and *Story of a Stone*) was written in the latter half of the 18th century and represents the peak of development in the traditional Chinese realistic novel; it is also a masterpiece of world literature. The author Cao Xueqin (1715?-1764) was born into a wealthy bureaucratic family in what is now Nanjing. In 1727 his father was dismissed from office on a charge of embezzlement and the family fortunes began to decline. The family moved to Beijing, and there Cao spent his last years in poverty, despite his talents as a poet and painter. *A*

---

[1] English translation published by FLP, 1973.
[2] English translation published by FLP, 1978.

Dream of Red Mansions is a product of his last years but it was left incomplete at the time of his early death. An 80-chapter text from his pen first circulated under the title *Story of a Stone*, and the novel's present title and form were the contribution of a later writer, Gao E, who added a final 40 chapters along the lines of the author's original intentions. In the tragic love stories of Jia Baoyu and his beautiful cousins Lin Daiyu and Xue Baochai and the changing fortunes of the aristocratic Jia family, the novel depicts the corruption of the feudal system and its inevitable collapse. The three main characters are powerfully portrayed: Jia Baoyu and Lin Daiyu, two rebels against feudal society, and Xue Baochai, a loyal upholder of orthodoxy. The author also brings to life a host of young women, including both young ladies and lowly maidservants, whose individual characters are drawn with meticulous care, and shows how each in their different fate suffered from the oppression of women inherent in the feudal system. There is also an extensive cast of male and female characters from all levels of society both inside and outside the large and powerful Jia clan. In language, *A Dream of Red Mansions* lifts the vernacular of the traditional Chinese novel to its highest point, skilfully combining colloquial and vulgar speech with highly refined poetry and prose in the literary language. The author also demonstrates extraordinary versatility in different modes of writing: narration, dialogue, poetry, descriptions of natural scenery and catalogue-like descriptions of the luxurious items of daily use in the Jia household. Altogether a model of the classic Chinese novel, it caused an immediate sensation on its appearance, and hand-written copies circulated for over 30 years.

Although afterwards it was repeatedly banned by the feudal bureaucracy, there was no way of preventing its circulation, and its influence on later Chinese literature is inestimable. With its enduring appeal to generations of young and old alike, this masterpiece is one of the best loved works in Chinese literary history.

Only slightly less famous is the 100-chapter Ming novel *Jin Ping Mei* (also known as *Golden Lotus*) by the pseudonymous "Laughing Scholar of Lanling". Taking its starting point from the love affair between Ximen Qing and Pan Jinlian (Golden Lotus) in *Outlaws of the Marsh*, it relates the history of the merchant Ximen Qing from his rise to fame and fortune in collaboration with the local officials to his final degradation and death. With brutal realism the novel describes his exploitation of the poor and oppression of women, and the cruelty and dissipation in the upper levels of society. Its incisive character studies and careful descriptions provided an important model for later Qing fiction.

Short Stories Three collections dominate the world of short fiction during the Ming and Qing. In the Ming Dynasty, many scholars created vernacular short stories in imitation of Song storytellers' scripts purely for private reading which have been passed down in collections such as the famous "Three Words" and "Two Astonishments". Continuing the tradition of stories of the marvellous, the Qing writer Pu Songling produced a one-volume collection of short stories in the literary language, *Strange Tales of Liaozhai*, a classic of short fiction.

"Three Words" is the collective name for three volumes of short stories compiled by Feng Menglong (1574-

1646), *Words to Instruct Men, Words to Warn Men* and *Words to Awaken Men*.[1] He collected and edited both authentic and imitation storytellers' scripts from the Song and Yuan, arranging 40 stories in each volume. Most of the stories are about contemporary urban life; there are stories about love and passion, attacking the oppression of women under the feudal system; stories praising friendship and condemning inconstancy; stories exposing the internal struggles of the ruling class; and stories condemning corrupt officials. While preserving the good qualities of the Song storytellers' scripts, the "Three Words" also are artistically more advanced: the themes are better focussed, the plots are more cleverly constructed, there is more attention to detail and the language is more polished.

Following the success of the "Three Words", the Ming writer Ling Mengchu wrote his own short stories in imitation of storytellers' scrips, compiling them in two volumes as *Astonishing and Miraculous Tales* I & II.[2] The two volumes contain altogether 78 stories and are known collectively as the "Two Astonishments". However, the "Two Astonishments" are inferior both ideologically and artistically to the "Three Words".

Strange Tales of Liaozhai[3] (also known as *Strange Stories from a Chinese Studio*) is a collection of almost 500 short stories by the Qing writer Pu Songling (1640-1715). An unsuccessful scholar under the old examina-

---

[1] English translations of some of these stories are included in *The Courtesan's Jewel Box*, FLP, 1981.

[2] English translations of some of these stories are included in *The Courtesan's Jewel Box*, FLP, 1981.

[3] Partial English translation in *Selected Tales of Liaozhai*, Panda Books, 1981.

tion system, he spent his life in poverty and had a good knowledge of conditions at the lower levels of society. Many of his stories describe the resistance offered by young lovers to interference by feudal moralists in their lives, the cruel oppression of the people by the feudal ruling class and malpractices in the examination system. The author adapts traditional tales of the marvellous, using foxes and ghosts from the nether world to reflect the real world and express his ideals, and creating bizarre and wonderful effects. He is particularly skilful in character portrayal, and under his pen a throng of beautiful, clever and passionate young women spring to life. Although he writes in the literary language, his style is fluent, witty and very polished.

Drama Ming and Qing drama can be divided into two kinds. One is the vari-drama inherited from the Yuan, which continued to be popular under the Ming and Qing but failed to register any outstanding achievement. The other was romance-drama, developed from the southern drama of the Yuan period, which pushed vari-drama from its dominant position in Yuan and early Ming. The southern drama was noted primarily for the beauty of its songs, which unlike in vari-drama could be sung by any of the leading characters, and its tuneful music, based on southern music and using the flute as its chief instrument. The songs and dialogue were delivered in the Wu dialect of the Suzhou region, where this form of drama first developed. Most of the plays are about love. The most famous romance-dramas are *Peony Pavilion*, from the Ming, and *Palace of Eternal Youth* and *Peach Blossom Fan* from the Qing.

The author of *Peony Pavilion*, Tang Xianzu (1550-1616), was a famous dramatist whose other works include

The Purple Flute, *The Purple Hairpin*, *The Tale of Handan* and *The Governor of the Southern Tributary State*. *Peony Pavilion* is the story of the love between Du Liniang and Liu Mengmei which triumphs over death, celebrating the lovers' spirit of resistance to feudal ethics and their search for individual liberation. The plot is a blend of fantasy and romance: Du Liniang dies after a lovesick dream but comes to life again to be reunited with her beloved. Her songs are particularly graceful and poetic and contribute largely to the play's great appeal.

The *Palace of Eternal Youth*[1] is by Hong Sheng (1645-1704), who wrote altogether nine plays of which only two survive. It describes the love between the Tang emperor Minghuang and Lady Yang, his favourite concubine, but while praising their love for having triumphed over death, the author also criticizes it for having brought calamity on the nation. By exposing the dissipation and corruption of the ruling class, the author enlarges the work's social significance. The play is well constructed and makes an impressive spectacle on stage, and the songs and musical accompaniment are particularly noted for their beauty. The appearance of *Palace of Eternal Youth* created a sensation and the script was frequently recopied and performed.

Peach Blossom Fan, by Kong Shangren (1648-1718) is far superior to *Palace of Eternal Youth* both ideologically and artistically and brings the development of Qing drama to its highest point. It weaves into the love story of the scholar Hou Chaozong and the courtesan Li Xiangjun the major historical events of the end of the Ming, exposing the internal conflicts and political corruption

---

[1] English translation published by FLP, 1980.

of the ruling class and showing the reasons for the fall of the Ming Dynasty. In a bold departure from the conventional pattern of plays of this kind, the author links the misfortunes of the lovers with the decline and fall of the country. This direct connection between love and politics is a daringly innovative step which had considerable influence on the later development of Chinese drama.

2. MODERN LITERATURE (1840-1919)

In the last years of the Qing Dynasty, imperialist aggression gradually transformed China's feudal society into a semi-feudal, semi-colonial society, and the Chinese people began their struggle against imperialism and feudalism. At the same time a wave of progressive literature appeared, reflecting the need for literature that served the current political struggle. Poetry, essays, fiction and drama all became more realistic and politicized, playing an important part in the bourgeois Enlightenment Movement in the second half of the 19th century, the Reform Movement of 1898 and the 1911 Revolution. The literature of this period and up to 1949 is known in China as Modern Literature.

(1) POETRY

Three progressive modern poets, Gong Zizhen, Huang Zunxian and Liu Yazi, represent the three stages of the bourgeois-democratic revolution.

Gong Zizhen (1792-1841), a leading activist in the Enlightenment Movement, was also the first to disturb the stagnating waters of late Qing poetry by developing a modernist style. The 600-odd poems he has left behind criticize current social evils directly and boldly, expressing intense dissatisfaction with the Qing court and deep sympathy for the suffering of the people. His poems reflect his interest in philosophy and thought and embody his fervent hopes for reform and his quest for intellectual liberation. In style he was most influenced by Qu Yuan and Li Bai, with whom he shares a vivid imagination and a grand and heroic manner. His language is very beautiful but unnecessarily obscure.

Huang Zunxian (1848-1905) was an active participant in the Reform Movement of 1898. He advocated a "revolution in poetry" along with other reformers such as Kang Youwei and Liang Qichao, arguing that contemporary poetry should be allowed to mention new inventions and other things that did not exist in the past, and that writing should imitate actual speech rather than classical poetry. In his own work he strove to accomplish a poetic revolution, for instance by using devices from classical prose writing and seeking inspiration from folk poetry. Between 1877 and 1894 he held a series of important diplomatic and consular posts in San Francisco, Tokyo, London and Singapore. His experiences overseas broadened his outlook and increased his knowledge, so that his poetry has an unusually wide range of subject matter including steamships, telegraph poles and other new phenomena from contemporary life and society. The major concern of his poetry, however, was China's destiny, and he wrote many narrative poems on major historical events. Poems such as "Lament for Lüshun", "Song of the Surrendered General", "Ballad of Taiwan" and "Song of General Du Liao" praise the loyal generals and soldiers of the 1894 Sino-Japanese War and satirize stupid and useless officials and the generals who surrendered to the enemy. His poems are collected in two volumes, *Poems from the Hut Within Men's Borders* (the name of his studio, from a famous poem by Tao Yuanming) and *Miscellaneous Poems on Japan*.

Liu Yazi (1887-1958), who was active in the bourgeois revolutionary movement, was the organizer and leader of the Southern Society, the first revolutionary literary society of the modern period. Other members of the society were the well-known poets Chen Qubing, Gao Xu and Su Manshu. An admirer of Gong Zizhen, Liu Yazi was opposed to mere imitation of classical models in poetry. His own poetic work is full of heroic revolutionary ardour, exposing social evils and recording the feats of national heroes and revolutionary martyrs. After the failure of the 1911 Revolution, he did not become demoralized as did the other Southern Society poets, but continued to write poetry in tune with the changing times. He was particularly adept at seven syllable line regulated verse and cut-short verse. His style is plain and simple but full of meaning.

Other reformers and revolutionaries of this period who wrote good verse include Wei Yuan, Lin Zexu, Kang Youwei, Tan Sitong and Qiu Jin.

(2) NON-FICTION PROSE

The need to propagate new ideas led to a revolution in prose style as well as poetry. After overcoming considerable initial opposition, the new style gradually became the mainstream of modern prose writing. Gong Zizhen, Wei Yuan, Yan Fu, Kang Youwei and Liang Qichao were the pioneers in writing reform.

Liang Qichao (1873-1929) was the most outstanding prose writer of his generation and the leading propagandist of the bourgeois Reform Movement of 1898. He advocated both a "revolution in poetry" and a "revolution in prose", and founded several newspapers and magazines to encourage the popularization of the new literary style. He believed that writing must be made more understandable for ordinary people and his own new prose was lucid and persuasive. *Young China Speaks* is one of his best known works. Here Liang Qichao praises in powerful language the inspiring role played by youth, expressing his ideas clearly and fluently. It enjoyed a great popularity for a time and many people joined the call for a new prose style following his example. Liang Qichao's new prose opened a path for the liberation of style in late Qing fiction and the vernacular literary movement of 1919.

Many of the 1911 revolutionaries regarded literature as a weapon in their struggle, such as Zhang Binglin (1869-1936), Chen Tianhua (1875-1905) and Zou Rong (1885-1905). Their articles and manifestoes are characterized by revolutionary ardour and fierce opposition to Qing rule. Zhang Binglin's writings were particularly militant, and his "Letter Disputing Kang Youwei" and "Denunciation of the Manchu" were widely circulated and very influential.

(3) FICTION

The late Qing Reform Movement was accompanied by a new type of fiction reflecting the demand for reform and denouncing current social evils. According to statistics, more than 1,000 novels appeared around this time, and also many treatises on the theory of fiction. The best of these novels are known as "the four great novels of exposure" (i.e. of social criticism): *The Bureaucrats: A Revelation, Strange Events of the Last Twenty Years, The Travels of Lao Can* and *A Flower in an Ocean of Sin*.

A Flower in an Ocean of Sin by Zeng Pu (1872-1935) is the best of the late Qing novels. It was originally planned to comprise 60 chapters, but the author died before it was complete. The plot concerns the love story of Jin Wenqing and the famous courtesan Fu Caiyun, and presents the political, economic and diplomatic situation of the end of the Qing through the lives of officials, scholars and writers in Beijing, Suzhou and abroad. The novel exposes the corruption of the Qing court and the aggressive ambitions of the imperialists. The author actively supports the democratic revolution and gives favourable portraits of Sun Yat-sen and other Chinese and foreign revolutionaries. The story is skilfully organized, but too many amorous anecdotes weaken its ideological value.

Apart from novels of exposure, late Qing fiction also included sentimental novels, known as the "mandarin duck and butterfly school" (mandarin ducks and butterflies are traditional symbols for romance and marriage) and scandal fiction, known as "black screen fiction". Although these novels were also to some extent critical of contemporary society, they nevertheless manifested its corruption within themselves and represent a degraded form of exposure fiction.

Increasing Sino-foreign contacts and the search for enlightment from the West led to the development of translation in late Qing China. The most famous early translators were Yan Fu and Lin Shu. Yan Fu (1853-1921) specialized in Western philosophical works, and his translation of Darwin's *The Origins of Species* had tremendous impact on Chinese thinking. Lin Shu (1852-1924) who specialized in fiction, translated over 100 novels, including *La Dame aux camélias* by Dumas *fils*, and *Uncle Tom's Cabin* by Harriet Beecher Stowe. These translations were all in the old literary language and were often substantially adapted. Almost 1,000 works of fiction from Russia, Japan, Britain, the United States, France and Germany were translated around this time, contributing substantially to the development of new fiction in the early 20th century.

(4) DRAMA

The dominant form of theatre from the 17th century to the 19th century was *kunqu*, a form of southern opera which gradually became the favourite of the court and the officials in the north. Originally a kind of folk opera from Kunshan, Jiangsu, it began to decline after its monopolization by the feudal literati and officials. *Kunqu* is characterised by elegant language, romantic plots and melodious tunes. Its decline was accompanied by the growth of more robust kinds of local operas.

Local Operas Developed from local folk song and balladry, local operas were comparatively close to the people. Their subject matter was drawn mostly from historical legends, folk stories and people's daily lives. The songs and spoken dialogue were both close to popular speech — plain, lively and easy to understand — and the music had a strong local flavour. Among the most popular old favourites of local opera are *Qin Xianglian* (a Hebei *bangzi* or clapper opera), *The Runaway Maid* (Cantonese Opera), *Love Under the Willows*[1] (Sichuan Opera), *Autumn River* (Sichuan Opera), *Ge Ma* (Hubei Opera) and *Beating the Princess* (Shanxi Opera). There are also many local operas about patriotic figures like Yue Fei and the generals of the Yang family.

Beijing Opera Beijing Opera is a form of opera that became popular in the capital in the mid-19th century. The music of Beijing Opera is based on two different types of tune-families, *erhuang* tunes from Anhui Opera and *xipi* tunes from Hubei Opera, along with additional elements from other kinds of opera including *kunqu*. For the last 100 years, Beijing Opera has been the dominant form of theatre throughout China. Many Beijing Opera stories are taken from the historical novels *Outlaws of the Marsh* and *Romance of the Three Kingdoms*, put together collectively by the performers. The most famous Beijing Operas include *The Empty City Ruse*, *The Gathering of Heroes*, *Women Generals of the Yang House*, *The King Parts from His Favourite*, *The Universal Sword*, *The Fisherman's Revenge*, *The Fork in the Road*, and *Havoc in Heaven*. Beijing Opera eventually won the favour of the Qing court and under court influence gradually drew away from the masses. In the latter part of the 19th century some progressive performers headed by Wang Xiaonong initiated a reform in Beijing Opera, adapting historical operas to apply to the present, criticizing current social evils and fostering a spirit of patriotism. The reformers also experimented with creating new works about contemporary life and society.

---

[1] English translation published by FLP, 1956.

The early 20th century also saw the introduction of Western drama into China. Known in Chinese as "new drama" or "civilized drama", it dispensed with the singing and stylized acting typical of traditional Chinese opera in favour of a realistic acting style and spoken dialogue. Some patriotic young people formed the Spring Willow Society to perform new drama, starting with an adaptation of *Uncle Tom's Cabin*. The participants later continued their activities in groups such as the Progressive Troupe, infusing new blood into Chinese theatre.

3. THE RISE OF REVOLUTIONARY LITERATURE (1919-1949)

The May 4th Patriotic Movement was a major turning point in Chinese history. Starting as a massive student demonstration on May 4, 1919 against feudalism and imperialism, it marked the appearance of the proletariat as a leading political force in Chinese history and the beginning of the New Democratic Movement. A new literature inspired by the May 4th slogans "Down with Confucius & Sons", "Support vernacular literature" and "Science and democracy", arose in opposition to the old feudal literature, and many progressive literary societies and periodicals made their appearance. The literature itself became known as "May 4th literature", and marks the beginning of a true modern literature in China.

The establishment of the Chinese Communist Party in 1921 provided the new literature movement with a firm leadership, and literature thenceforth played a more conscious and conspicuous role in the revolutionary cause. A host of revolutionary writers, such as Lu Xun, Guo

Moruo, Mao Dun, Ba Jin, Lao She and Cao Yu, reflected the current struggle in their works, promoting directly and indirectly the development of the revolutionary movement, and adding new treasures to the storehouse of Chinese literature.

(1) LITERATURE OF THE MAY 4TH PERIOD

The May 4th Literary Revolution The revolution in modern Chinese literature had its beginnings in 1915 when the progressive intellectuals Chen Duxiu and Li Dazhao, writing in the magazine *New Youth*, called for the reform of Chinese literature as part of their opposition to feudal culture and support for democracy and science. In an article entitled "On the Literary Revolution", Chen Duxiu condemned the corrupt feudal aristocratic literature of the past and demanded a new realistic, popular national literature. This article marks the formal beginning of the Literary Revolution. In 1917 the bourgeois writer and scholar Hu Shi recommended reforms in the language and form of literature in an article entitled "Some Suggestions for the Reform of Literature". In 1918, on the eve of the May 4th Movement, Lu Xun, the forerunner of the Literary Revolution, published his first short story, "A Madman's Diary". The story ruthlessly exposes the cannibalistic nature of feudal ethics. The patriotic anti-feudal, anti-imperialist demonstrations that began on May 4, 1919 brought about a radical change in Chinese literature, which had been stagnant since the failure of the 1911 Revolution. Fiction and drama, formerly regarded as mere entertainment, were elevated to the status of literature proper, and the vernacular replaced the literary language as the main vehicle for literary expression. The major theme of the new literature was opposition to feudalism and imperialism, and new topics included the sufferings of the peasants and their struggle against feudalism, and the intellectuals' opposition to feudal ethics and their search for personal liberation and free love. The introduction of foreign literature, especially progressive literature from Russia and Europe, was also an important factor in the Literary Revolution. The two major works of the twenties are *Call to Arms*, a collection of short stories by Lu Xun, and *The Goddesses*, a collection of poems by Guo Moruo. The new literary societies and periodicals were also an important achievement of the Literary Revolution.

The Main Literary Societies and Their Authors The May 4th Movement was accompanied by a great flowering of literary societies and periodicals. More than 100 literary societies and several hundred literary periodicals were founded between 1921 and 1925. The earliest and most influential of these organizations were the Literary Research Society and the Creation Society.

The Literary Research Society was founded in Beijing in January 1921 by a group of 12 people including Mao Dun (then known as Shen Yanbing), Zheng Zhenduo, Ye Shengtao and Wang Tongzhao. Its main publications were *Short Story Monthly*, *Literature Ten-Daily* and *Poetry* (a monthly), and a literary series comprising 125 titles. Branch societies were established in several large cities and published their own journals. The Literary Research Society advocated "literature for life's sake", opposing both entertainment literature and art for art's sake. Adopting Western techniques of realism for the exposure and criticism of contemporary society, its members created many important literary works. They also translated and reviewed many famous realistic writers from abroad. Mao Dun, Zheng Zhenduo, Ye Shengtao, Bing Xin, Zhu Ziqing, Wang Tongzhao, Lu Yan and Xu Dishan were its best-known writers.

The Creation Society was established in July 1921 in Tokyo by Chinese students in Japan, including Guo Moruo, Yu Dafu, Cheng Fangwu and Tian Han. The society published about a dozen periodicals during the twenties, including *Creation Quarterly*, *Creation Weekly* and *Creation Daily*. The Creation writers held that the main function of literature was self-expression, and their own work is characterized by originality and subjectivism. They rejected the orthodox tradition in Chinese literature in favour of the romantic tradition in China and the West. Initially the Creation writers were believers in art for art's sake, but in the mid-twenties they revised their position and proposed the creation of proletarian literature. Guo Moruo, Yu Dafu, Zheng Boqi and Cheng Fangwu were the most important Creation writers.

The Tatler Society, the Unnamed Society, the Sunken Bell Society and the Crescent Moon Society were also influential in the twenties.

Lu Xun and His *Call to Arms* Lu Xun is the penname of Zhou Shuren (1881-1936), the founder of modern Chinese literature and its most outstanding writer. As a child he received a traditional education in the Chinese classics, but was introduced to modern Western scientific thinking in his later schooling, and was deeply influenced by Darwin's theory of evolution. He went to Japan to study medicine in 1902, but four years later, however, he abandoned medicine for literature, believing that the most important task for China was renovating the national spirit, and that literature was the most effective weapon for doing this. After returning to China, he found employment as a teacher and educational administrator, and at the same time continued to write and translate foreign literature into Chinese. In 1918 he became an editor of *New Youth* and his famous short story, "A Madman's Diary" was published in *New Youth* the same year. In 1924 he was one of the main contributors to the *Tatler*, and in the following year he founded a new weekly, *The Wilderness*. He was also an active supporter of the student protest movement of 1925. In October 1927, after short stays in Xiamen and Guangzhou, he settled in Shanghai where he remained for the rest of his days. The greater part of Lu Xun's writings date from the period 1918-1927: *Call to Arms*[1] and *Wandering*[2] (short stories), *Hot Air, The Grave, Bad Luck* and *Bad Luck (II)*[3] (satirical and other essays), *Wild Grass*[4] (prose poems) and *Dawn Blossoms Plucked at Dusk*[5] (reminiscences).

Call to Arms, comprising 14 short stories written between 1918 and 1922, is the foundation stone of modern Chinese literature. It gives a broad picture of Chinese society from around the 1911 Revolution to the May 4th Movement, depicting the states of mind of different classes of people in the countryside and towns suffering under imperialist and feudal oppression, and creating imperishable portraits of peasants and wavering intellectuals. Lu Xun was above all a ruthless critic of feudal

---

[1] English translation published by FLP, 1981.
[2] English translation published by FLP, 1981.
[3] A selection of these essays in English translation has been published under the title *Lu Xun: Selected Works*, FLP, 1980.
[4] English translation published by FLP, 1974.
[5] English translation published by FLP, 1976.

ethics and the feudal gentry, and his brilliant exposure of the cannibalistic nature of the old ethics in "A Madman's Diary" was an important contribution to contemporary thinking. The masterpiece of *Call to Arms* is "The True Story of Ah Q", which has been translated into 40 foreign languages. "Kong Yiji", "Medicine" and "My Old Home", also from *Call to Arms,* and "Regrets for the Past" and "The New-Year Sacrifice" from *Wandering* are also outstanding.

Lu Xun's prose style was a unique creation which borrowed both from Chinese classical writing and modern Western fiction. His remarkably terse and trenchant use of language, biting satire, powerful symbolism and close attention to compositional structure created an entirely new kind of fiction in China. His ability to describe Chinese reality with Western literary techniques was a great contribution to the development of modern Chinese literature.

Guo Moruo and *The Goddesses* Guo Moruo (1892-1978) was an outstanding modern Chinese writer, poet, historian and social activist. In his childhood he received a traditional education, but in 1914 he went to Japan to study medicine, fired with the ambition of building China into a rich and powerful nation. During his studies abroad he came in contact with a wide range of Western literature and bourgeois democratic ideas. After returning to China he devoted himself to the new literature movement and as a leading member of the Creation Society declared that the Literary Revolution should be transformed into a revolutionary literature. He became a Marxist in 1924 after translating Marxist works. In 1926 he took part in the joint Kuomintang-Communist Northern Expedition against feudal warlord rule, and in the

Communist-led August 1st Uprising in Nanchang the following year. In 1927 he also joined the Chinese Communist Party. The persecution of Left-wing writers by the Kuomintang in the late twenties forced him into self-exile in Japan, where he stayed until the outbreak of the War of Resistance Against Japan in 1937.

In spite of his social involvements, Guo Moruo was very prolific throughout the twenties. He began writing new poetry in 1918, and his first collection, *The Goddesses*, was published in 1921. His other works for this period include *Starry Skies*, a collection of poems; *Vase*, *Vanguard* and *Restoration* (poetry); *Pagoda* (short stories and plays); *Below the Horizon* and *Olives* (short stories and essays); and *Fallen Leaves* (short stories). He also wrote several historical plays, including *Nie Ying*, *Wang Zhaojun* and *Zhuo Wenjun*.

The Goddesses[1] was the first and most important collection of new poetry and had an enormous influence in the history of modern Chinese literature. The poems themselves are highly romantic and patriotic. "The Nirvana of the Feng and Huang", for instance, relates the story of the *feng* and *huang* (the phoenix cock and hen) who cast themselves into a fire and are reborn in the flames. The fate of these mythical birds symbolizes the destruction of old China and the poet's old self and the rebirth of the new China and the poet's new self. There are also many poems exalting personal liberation and supporting socialist ideology. Guo Moruo's style is grand and heroic, deeply emotional, inventive and imaginative. His adoption of free verse revolutionized

---

[1] English translation published by FLP, 1978.

the writing of poetry in China, setting it free from the traditional strict rules of prosody.

Other Important Writers and Their Works The May 4th period was a particularly fruitful time in the history of Chinese literature. Ye Shengtao, Yu Dafu, Zhu Ziqing and Bing Xin are among the more influential writers of the time.

Ye Shengtao (b. 1894) began writing fiction on the eve of the May 4th Movement and was one of the most accomplished of the Literary Research Society writers. During the late teens and the twenties he wrote over 70 short stories, which have been published in three volumes, *Estranged*, *Fire* and *Below the Line*. His favourite topic is the boring, meaningless life of small-town intellectuals and petty-bourgeoisie which he subjects to merciless criticism, but he also wrote with sympathy about the life and sufferings of workers. Ye Shengtao was the earliest writer to specialize in children's literature. His best-known work in this field is a collection of short stories for children entitled *Scarecrow*.[1] His one and only novel, *Ni Huanzhi*,[2] written in 1928, describes the historical period from the 1911 Revolution to the end of the twenties through the life of a petty-bourgeois intellectual. It is one of the earliest and best novels in modern Chinese literature.

Yu Dafu (1896-1945), a leading member of the Creation Society, also studied in Japan as a young man, and his early stories are mostly autobiographical. "Sinking" is a typical early work depicting the loneliness of a for-

---

[1] English translation published by FLP, 1978.
[2] English translation published as *Schoolmaster Ni Huanzhi* by FLP, 1978.

eign student in a strange country. Yu Dafu's early stories are notable for their unusual frankness in dealing with the problems of young people and caused an immediate sensation when they were published. As the momentum of the revolutionary movement increased, the author's field of vision also broadened to take in the misfortunes of the labouring people, inspiring excellent short stories such as "Intoxicating Spring Nights" and "A Humble Sacrifice".[1]

Zhu Ziqing (1898-1948) was one of the earliest members of the Literary Research Society to write new poetry, and his long lyric poem, "Destruction", made a considerable impact on its publication in 1923. His main fame, however, is as a prose writer. Some of his essays, such as "The White Man — God's Proud Son" and "The Price of a Life — Seventy Cents" describe major social problems; his lyrical essays, such as "My Father's Back" and "The Lotus Pool by Midnight"[2] have also been highly praised for their graceful style.

Bing Xin is the pen-name of Xie Wanying (b. 1900), an important May 4th poet and short story writer. The main topics of her short stories are the family, children and social problems. Among her best-known works are "The Superman", "I Alone So Pale and Wan", "Zhuanghong's Sisters" and "Two Families". From 1923 to 1926 she studied in the U.S., where she wrote two collections of poetry, *The Stars* and *Spring Waters*, and essays for children about her travels and experiences under the title *Letters to My Young Readers*. Despite her mistaken belief in "universal love", Bing Xin's works reflect her

---

[1] English translations published in *Chinese Literature*, 1957, 3.

[2] English translations in *Chinese Literature*, 1958, 1.

strong sense of patriotism and justice. Her descriptions of nature are particularly vivid and fresh.

From Literary Revolution to Revolutionary Literature After the founding of the Chinese Communist Party in 1921 and the rise of the workers' and peasants' movement, the proletariat began to take the lead in the new literature movement. In 1923, Deng Zhongxia, Yun Daiying, Qu Qiubai and Jiang Guangchi, all Party members, published an article urging writers to adopt a Marxist approach to literature. Criticizing the advocates of feudal restoration and art for art's sake, they demanded a literature of social reform reflecting the hopes and needs of China's masses. As the revolutionary movement progressed, many writers and young readers personally took part in the revolutionary struggle, and their thinking became increasingly revolutionized. In 1925 Mao Dun wrote an important article on the need for a proletarian literature, followed in 1926 by Guo Moruo's "Revolution and Literature" and "The Consciousness of Writers and Artists", two articles promoting "literature that speaks for the oppressed classes" and "literature that sympathizes with proletarian socialism and realism". Lu Xun also gave famous lectures such as "The Literature of a Revolutionary Age" in this period. These activities were of great significance in the history of modern Chinese literature, preparing the conditions for the rise of the Left-wing literary movement of the thirties.

(2) REVOLUTIONARY LITERATURE IN THE THIRTIES

The League of Left-Wing Writers and Proletarian Literature After the failure of the First Revolutionary

Civil War against northern warlord rule in 1927, the bourgeoisie betrayed the revolution, leaving the Communist Party to continue the struggle alone. Battlelines were also sharply drawn between Left and Right-wing writers, and Shanghai became the camp of Left-wing writers like Guo Moruo, Cheng Fangwu, Feng Naichao, Qian Xingcun and Yang Hansheng. Among those who flocked to Shanghai in those years were some writers who were returning to literature after having taken part in the revolutionary struggle, some writers who had been influenced by the international proletarian literary movement during their studies abroad, and some revolutionary intellectuals who had previously been engaged in practical political work. In the winter of 1927 Jiang Guangchi, Qian Xingcun and Hong Lingfei founded the Sun Society, an organization for revolutionary literature. At the beginning of 1928, the Sun Society and the reorganized Creation Society renewed the call for proletarian literature in *Creation Monthly* and *Sun Monthly,* clearing the path for the Leftwing literary movement of the 1930s. Their translations and studies of Marxist social science and their adoption of Marxist literary theory to guide the literary movement, emphasizing the class nature of literature and its propaganda function, played an important role in maintaining morale at a time when the revolution was at a low ebb. However, because their grasp of Marxist theory was still inadequate, their thinking tended to be one-sided and dogmatic, and as a consequence they not only made mistakes in their analysis of the revolutionary situation but some of their literary demands were misguided. Lu Xun, among others, became the target for their criticism, and the controversies they provoked in the new literature camp lasted for more than a year. The controversy had the effect of strengthening the study and research of Marxist literary theory and forming an ideological basis for unity. The suppression of writers by the Kuomintang government also spurred the revolutionary writers to seek unity.

In March 1930 the Chinese League of Left-Wing Writers was formally established in Shanghai, on the general programme that literature must serve the revolutionary cause. A standing committee consisting of Lu Xun, Feng Naichao, Xia Yan, Qian Xingcun, Tian Han, Zheng Boqi and Hong Lingfei was elected. Mao Dun and Zhou Yang also took part in the League's activities when they returned from Japan soon after. Lu Xun, who by this time had become the acknowledged leader of the revolutionary literary movement, gave an important speech at the League's inaugural meeting, summing up the lessons of the immediate past and raising many key problems in the revolutionary literature movement, including the current "Leftist" tendency. League branches and study groups were also set up in Beiping (modern Beijing), Tianjin, Guangzhou and Tokyo. The KMT government continued to intimidate writers with censorship, jail and execution, but the League writers refused to abandon their struggle, and over the next few years they managed to publish over a dozen open and underground literary periodicals, such as *The Dipper, Literature Monthly, Sprouts Monthly* and *Literary Guide,* and set up study groups on Marxist literary theory. Through these organs they carried out a resolute struggle against reactionary literary factions and misguided theories, circulated their own creative work and fostered a new generation of revolutionary writers. Although some

"Left" defects and errors still existed in the League's work, it made an important contribution to the development of revolutionary literature and occupies an important position in the history of modern Chinese literature.

Alongside the proletarian literary movement and influenced by it were a group of progressive democratic writers. Their publications included *Literature* and *Literature Quarterly,* edited by Zheng Zhenduo and Wang Tongzhao, and *Literature Monthly* and *Literary Grove,* edited by Ba Jin and Jin Yi, along with several important literary series.

The Formation of a National United Front Against Japan On September 18, 1931, the Japanese imperialists seized the city of Shenyang and proceeded to occupy the three northeastern provinces. When the Chinese Communist Party made its call for an anti-Japanese national united front in 1935, the literary world enthusiastically responded. At the beginning of 1936, the League of Left-Wing Writers announced its dissolution, and some of its former members such as Zhou Libo and Zhou Yang proposed a united front in literature under the slogan "national defence literature". This proposal gained wide support, but in April the same year, in order to remedy a "lack of clarity" in this formulation, Lu Xun, Mao Dun and Feng Xuefeng put forward another slogan, "mass literature of the national revolutionary war". In October 1936, Lu Xun, Guo Moruo, Mao Dun, Ba Jin, Ye Shengtao, Bing Xin and others issued a "Writers' Manifesto on the United Resistance Against Aggression and on Freedom of Speech", which laid the ground for the formation of a united front in literature.

The Achievements of Revolutionary Literature in the Thirties The development of the Left-wing literary movement encouraged a great upsurge in writing in the thirties. The most conspicuous characteristic of the new writing in this period was the introduction of such topics as landlord and capitalist exploitation and oppression of workers and peasants, the workers' and peasants' rising consciousness and struggles, and the activities of revolutionaries.

Lu Xun and his later works. In the last nine years of his life Lu Xun wrote a large number of prose works which altogether formed 10 volumes: *And That's That, Three Leisures, Two Hearts, Mixed Dialects, False Liberty, Pseudo-Frivolous Talk, Fringed Literature, Essays of Qiejieting, Essays of Qiejieting (II)* and *The Last Essays of Qiejieting* (the last-mentioned compiled posthumously).[1] The essays covered a broad range of topics but the basic theme is the same, criticism of imperialism and the activities of KMT reactionaries and their running dogs in the world of literature. Most were in the form of short satirical essays known as *zawen,* a literary form that Lu Xun brought to a new height of perfection; there were also jottings, reviews, political essays, letters, biographical sketches, literary criticism and so on. Especially in the satirical essays, Lu Xun uses his brilliantly incisive style to devastating effect.

Lu Xun's essays occupy an important place in the history of modern Chinese literature. They constitute an authentic artistic record of modern Chinese life and thought, describing the great clashes between the newly arisen Chinese proletariat and the forces of feudalism and imperialism in the twenties and thirties and providing a detailed and comprehensive portrait of the whole age.

---

[1] A selection of these essays in English translation has been published in *Lu Xun: Selected Works,* FLP, 1980.

Mao Dun. Mao Dun was the pen-name of Shen Yanbing (1896-1981), a pioneer in modern Chinese progressive culture and a great revolutionary writer. After finishing the preparatory course at Beijing University, he took a job as proofreader and then editor in the Commercial Press in Shanghai, one of China's biggest publishing houses. He adopted literature as his profession during the May 4th Movement. As one of the main founders of the Literary Research Society, he was the chief editor for several years of *Short Story Monthly* and other Literary Research Society periodicals. In 1928 he published his first novel, *The Canker,* followed shortly by another novel, *Rainbow,* and two short novels, *The Road* and *Three Companions.*[1] Mao Dun's most fruitful period was from 1931 to 1937, when he wrote the outstanding short stories, "The Shop of the Lin Family", "Spring Silkworms", "Autumn Harvest" and "Winter Ruin"[2] and his most famous work, the novel *Midnight.*[3] *Midnight* is the most outstanding realistic novel in modern Chinese literature. Against the background of the industrial city of Shanghai in the early thirties, the novel charts the conflicts between the national industrial capitalist Wu Sunfu and the comprador financial capitalist Zhao Botao, in a masterly analysis of the complex contradictions in Chi-

---

[1] In contemporary Chinese literary criticism, fiction is categorized into three kinds according to length: short, medium, long. These categories correspond to the short story, the long short story or short novel, and the novel. The long short story or short novel is regarded as a distinct category, and continues to be a popular literary form up to the present day.

[2] Translations of these short stories are included in the selection of Mao Dun's short stories published under the title *Spring Silkworms and Other Stories,* FLP, 1979.

[3] English translation published by FLP, 1979.

nese society at that time. In Wu Sunfu, the author creates a typical representative figure of native Chinese capitalism. Apart from the main characters and plot, the author unfolds a broad picture of Chinese social life in vivid detail. The intricate structure of the many plots and subplots is handled with meticulous care, testifying to the author's skill in narrative technique and composition. Mao Dun was also a prolific essayist. While his fiction is chiefly the portrayal of an age through individual characters and their fate, the essays reveal social evils through direct depiction and biting satire on human relationships.

Ba Jin. Ba Jin is the pen-name of Li Feigan (b. 1904). As a young man he went to study in France and began his literary career in 1927 while he was still abroad. Most of his important works date from the late twenties and the thirties, such as *Destruction, New Life, Love, A Trilogy* (*Fog, Rain, Lightning*) and *The Torrent* (*Family, Spring, Autumn*), and the short story collections *Revenge, Glory* and *The General*. *The Torrent* is his best-known work, especially its first volume, *Family*.[1] Through the behind-the-scenes description of life in a bureaucrat landlord family, he scathingly criticizes the shameless degradation of the feudal landlord class and the hypocrisy and cruelty of feudal ethics, and praises the awakening and resistance of young students during the early May 4th Movement. The historically inevitable collapse of the feudal system is clearly presented. Based on his own life, *Family* is filled with incident and lively, believable characters, and its passionate sincerity has moved the hearts of generations of young people. The novel *Fire* was written during the War of Resistance Against Japan,

---

[1] English translation published by FLP, 1978.

and describes how Shanghai youth took part in the national struggle after the outbreak of hostilities. In the forties Ba Jin wrote several more novels, including *The Garden of Rest, Cold Nights* and *Ward Number Four,* and almost 100 short stories. Apart from fiction, Ba Jin has also written several volumes of essays, travel notes and reminiscences, such as *Memoirs, Short Conversations, Notes on a Journey* and *Confessions of a Life.*

Lao She. Lao She is the pen-name of Shu Qingchun (1899-1966), the son of a poor Manchu family in Beijing. From his own childhood experiences Lao She had an intimate knowledge of the lives of impoverished city dwellers. His career as a writer dates from 1924, shortly after the May 4th Movement, when he was teaching in England. At this time he produced three satirical novels, *The Philosophy of Lao Zhang, Master Zhao Says,* and *The Two Ma's.* After he returned to China in 1930, he continued to earn his living as a teacher and write at the same time. In the thirties he wrote a large number of short stories, collected in *Going to the Market, Sea of Cherries* and *Clams and Seaweeds,* the novels *Cat City, Divorce* and *Camel Xiangzi* and a short novel, *My Life.* His best-known work is *Camel Xiangzi,*[1] also known as *Rickshaw Boy,* which describes the tragic fate of a rickshaw puller. Written with deep sympathy for the oppressed, this moving work is a devastating indictment of the old society. The author draws freely on the rich and colourful dialect of his native Beijing, creating a vivid and authentic style. In the forties Lao She also wrote plays, drum-songs and poetry as well as fiction. His best-known work of this

---

[1] English translation published by FLP, 1981.

period is the novel *Four Generations Under One Roof*, describing life in Beijing under enemy occupation.

Cao Yu. Cao Yu is the pen-name of Wan Jiabao (b. 1910). His interest in the theatre dates from his middle-school days when he read widely in Chinese and foreign literature, including drama, and took part in amateur theatricals. His first full length play, *Thunderstorm*,[1] was performed in 1934, causing a great sensation in the theatre. In 1936 he finished another four-act play, *Sunrise*.[2] These two plays reflect the corruption of semi-feudal, semi-colonial upper class society in the cities. *Thunderstorm* compresses into the space of one day the complex 30-year history of involvement between two families, the bourgeois Zhou family and the servant Lu family. In the tragedy that ensues from their illicit relationships, the author reveals the dissipation and meanness of the bourgeoisie. Each character in the relatively small cast is carefully and clearly drawn, and their tragic fate is deeply moving. *Sunrise* is about Chinese urban life in the early thirties under the influence of the capitalist world depression, and shows the forces of darkness before the sunrise. The social life depicted in *Sunrise* is broader than in *Thunderstorm*, and the former is also simpler in style and more artistically effective. Cao Yu's wartime play, *Beijing Man*, on the disintegration of the old feudal family system, was even more advanced artistically and ideologically. These three plays have been frequently performed over the years, remaining an unfading attraction and testimony to the excellence of drama since the May 4th Movement.

---

[1] English translation published by FLP, 1978.
[2] English translation published by FLP, 1978.

Other important writers and works. In addition to the titles mentioned above, many other fine works of fiction, drama, poetry and essays were produced in the thirties, spreading revolutionary thinking and making a great contribution to the development of modern Chinese literature.

Two notable playwrights were Tian Han and Hong Shen. Tian Han (1898-1968) wrote a large number of plays about the life and struggles of workers and peasants and anti-Japanese resistance. His early works include the play *Death of a Star,* on the difficulties of actors in the old society. This was followed by several plays on the current struggle, such as *Plum Rain, Moonlight Serenade of 1932, Song of Returning Spring* and *Flood.* Tian Han was also the author of China's first Western-style opera, *Storm on the Yangtze River,* and the traditional opera, *The Fisherman's Song.* Hong Shen (1894-1955) was the author of the one-act play *Wukui Bridge,* the three-act play *Fragrant Rice* and the four-act play in Sichuan dialect, *Bao Dexing. Wukui Bridge* was one of the earliest plays on the peasant struggle.

Jiang Guangchi (1901-1931) was a pioneer in revolutionary fiction. His short novel *Des Sans-culottes* describes the workers' uprising in Shanghai in 1927 and his novel *The Roaring Land* introduces for the first time in fiction the subject of the peasants' revolutionary struggle under the leadership of the Chinese Communist Party.

Rou Shi (1901-1931) was the author of two important works, *Threshold of Spring* (1929),[1] a novel on the life of young intellectuals, and the outstanding short story,

---

[1] English translation published by FLP, 1980.

"The Hired Wife" (1930), on the tragic experience of a poor woman in the countryside.

Hu Yepin (1903-1931) was the author of *To Moscow* (1929), a novel on a woman's quest for a meaningful life, and *Light Lies Before Us* (1930), about a young couple's love and search for revolution.

Zhang Tianyi (b. 1906) has been popular among readers for many years for his breadth of subject matter, distinctive style and courage in facing up to reality. Among his works are the short stories "From Emptiness to Fullness", "Little Peter", "The Honey-Bee" and "Spring Breeze", the short novel *The Qingming Festival*, and the novels *A Journal of Hell*, *One Year* and *In the City*. He also wrote children's stories, such as *Big Lin and Little Lin*[1] and *King Baldy*.

Ye Zi (1912-1939) is known for his short stories "Harvest"[2] and "A Night in a Mountain Village" and a short novel, *Stars*.

After the September 18th Incident of 1931 many young writers fled from the Japanese-occupied northeastern provinces to other parts of China, nursing an intense desire for revenge and recovery of their homeland. Among many works on the anti-Japanese resistance in the northeast, Xiao Jun's *Village in August* and Xiao Hong's *Field of Life and Death* had the greatest impact.

Two important poets of the thirties were Yin Fu and Zang Kejia. Yin Fu (1909-1931) was an outstanding poet in the history of modern Chinese literature. He wrote many inspirational political poems and battle hymns, such as "Labour Day, 1929", "Revolution" and "Words in

---

[1] English translation published by FLP, 1965.

[2] English translation published in the collection of the same name, FLP, 1979.

Blood" on the struggles of revolutionaries and workers. Zang Kejia (b. 1905) mostly wrote songs of the countryside, describing the hard life of workers and peasants in the old society. His poems of the thirties are in two collections, *The Brand* (1934) and *The Black Hand of Sin* (1936). In 1936 he also wrote an excellent long poem on the quest of an intellectual for a progressive ideology, called "Self-Portrait".

The thirties is also famous for its essays and other non-fiction prose such as reportage. After Lu Xun, the most important satirical essays were written by Qu Qiubai (1899-1935), in the collections *Literary Miscellanea, Idle Talk and Other Essays* and *Literary Miscellanea (II)*. The most outstanding achievement in reportage literature at this time is Xia Yan's *Indentured Labourers*, which accurately portrays the inhuman life of women workers in a Japanese spinning factory in Shanghai and the evils of the imperialist colonialist system. Its powerful and original style gives it a strong artistic appeal.

(3) LITERATURE DURING THE FIRST PART OF THE WAR OF RESISTANCE AGAINST JAPAN (1937-1942)

The Founding of the Writers' Anti-Aggression Association In July 1937 the Japanese imperialists launched a full-scale invasion of China, and the Kuomintang and the Chinese Communist Party joined forces in order to counter enemy aggression. After the fall of Shanghai and Nanjing in 1938, the progressive writers gathered in Wuhan, where they established the National Chinese Writers' Anti-Aggression Association. Forty-five people were elected as council members, including Guo Moruo,

Mao Dun, Ba Jin, Lao She, Xia Yan, Zheng Zhenduo and Ding Ling; Zhou Enlai was elected an honorary council member and Lao She was elected secretary-general. A writers' correspondence network and local branches were set up by the Association, which also published its own journal, *Resistance Literature,* to organize writers to serve the resistance by going to the countryside and to the front. Most of the literature in this early period of the war consisted of short popular works hastily produced to meet the urgent needs of the resistance movement.

The Literary Movement in the Base Areas In 1936 the Red Army completed its arduous Long March and set up headquarters in north Shaanxi. In the same year, the Chinese Literary Association was founded in north Shaanxi with Ding Ling as its chairman. After the outbreak of the War of Resistance Against Japan and the formation of a Kuomintang-Communist united front, the Red Army was transformed into the Eighth Route Army operating in the Shaanxi-Gansu-Ningxia border region (known for convenience as Shaan-Gan-Ning) with its headquarters in Yan'an. In 1938, the Shaan-Gan-Ning National Salvation Association of Cultural Circles was set up in Yan'an, with Ai Siqi and Ke Zhongping in charge. Under the leadership of the Cultural Association and the general political department of the Eighth Route Army, literature and art troupes such as the Resistance Literary and Art Troupe, the Northwest War-Zone Service Troupe and the Experimental Drama Troupe were sent to work at the front line and in the countryside. Among the literary magazines published under extremely difficult conditions during this period were *Literary Battle-Front, Yan'an Literature, Northwest Literature* and *Popular Literature.* There were also a village writers' and performers' drama movement and "A Day in Central Hebei" reportage literature movement. Urged by the mass arts movement to study folk literature, many authors remodelled their poetic style to resemble folk song, bringing new poetry closer to the masses. In some areas discussions were held on creating new operas on the basis of *yangge,* a popular song and dance form in the north China countryside. The Lu Xun Academy of the Arts was established in Yan'an in 1938 and Lu Xun Colleges of Literature and the Arts were founded in central China and southeast Shanxi, to train large numbers of cadres in the cause of Chinese revolutionary art and literature. The development of the literary movement in the base areas behind the lines prepared for the arrival of a new period in revolutionary literature.

Major Authors and Their Works:

The poetry of Ai Qing and Tian Jian. Ai Qing is the pen-name of Jiang Haicheng (b. 1910). His first volume of poetry, *Dayanhe* (1936), which describes his love for peasants and the land and his bourgeois-democratic revolutionary ideology, brought him immediate recognition in the literary world. In the early years of the War of Resistance Against Japan he turned his attention to the struggle for national liberation. His poems from this time, were collected under the titles *The North, Facing the Sun, He Dies a Second Time, News of the Dawn,* and *The Torch.* The long poem *He Dies a Second Time,* about a wounded soldier who returns to the front line, is full of patriotic feeling. In 1941 Ai Qing went to Yan'an, where he wrote poems such as "Mao Zedong", "Let Us Proclaim to the

World", "Arise and Defend the Border Areas", "Drilling in the Snow", and "What the Sun Says", warmly praising the new age and new life. Ai Qing's poems are original, imaginative, bold and deeply felt. His contribution to the development of free verse is particularly noteworthy.[1] Tian Jian is the pen-name of Tong Tianjian (b. 1916), a prolific poet of the war period. His long lyric poem, "To the Fighters", a battle cry of the people's resistance, became one of the best known war poems of its time. Tian Jian went to Yan'an in 1938 and also worked in the Shanxi-Chahar-Hebei base area, writing poems on the people's lives and struggles in the base areas. His poems had considerable impact, their short lines and heavy rhythms creating an atmosphere of great power and militancy.

Other important works of this period are Ke Zhongping's long narrative poem "The Border Defence Army", Zang Kejia's long poem, "Flowers on an Old Tree", He Qifang's collection *Night Songs* and Guang Weiran's long poem *Yellow River Cantata*, a kind of national epic.

Novels by two Sichuan writers, Sha Ting and Ai Wu. Sha Ting (b. 1904) began his career as a writer in 1931, and his works on land revolution and village life under warlord rule attracted immediate attention. The collection of short stories written in 1940, *In the Qixiangju Teahouse,* is one of his best-known early works. He also wrote three novels in the early forties, *Prospecting for Gold, Beasts at Bay* and *Notes on a Journey Home*. These tightly constructed works have a deep underlying meaning and are rich in local colour. A prolific writer, Sha

---

[1] A selection of poems by Ai Qing translated into English under the title *Ai Qing: Selected Poems* has been published by FLP, 1982.

Ting was an important literary figure during the war years. Ai Wu (b. 1904) began to write in 1931. His first short story collections were *Notes on a Southern Journey* and *Nights in a Southern Land*, on local customs and life in the Yunnan border region. During the War Against Japan he returned to Sichuan where he wrote the short stories collected in *Autumn Harvest* and *The Wasteland*. The former is mostly about the changes in people's thinking and social customs since the war, while the latter exposes the underhand dealings of the wartime Kuomintang bureaucracy. His novel *The Fertile Plain* is one of his major works of this period and one of the best works in modern Chinese literature on peasant life.

Xia Yan and other playwrights. Xia Yan is the penname of Shen Duanxian (b. 1900). He was one of the founders of the League of Left-Wing Dramatists in the thirties, working mainly in film and modern drama. Among his fine pre-war plays are *The Story of Qiu Jin* and *Under Shanghai Eaves*. During the War Against Japan he wrote plays on the theme of resistance to Japan such as *City of Sorrow*, *Fragrant Grass Along the Horizon* and his two best-known plays of the period, *Fortress of the Heart* and *The Fascist Baccillus*. Other important works of the early war period are Yu Ling's *Shanghai Nights*, Chen Baichen's *Wedding March*, Yang Hansheng's historical play *Annals of the Kingdom of Heaven*, Ouyang Yuqian's historical play, *The Loyal Prince Li Xiucheng*, Ding Xilin's *Three Dollars, National Currency* and Wu Zuguang's *Return on a Snowy Night*.

Guo Moruo and *Qu Yuan*. After the beginning of the war, Guo Moruo returned to China from Japan. As a contribution to the war effort, he wrote or revised earlier versions of six historical plays, all with a lesson for the present: *Twin Flowers*,[1] *Qu Yuan*,[1] *Tiger Tally*,[1] *Gao Jianli*, *The Peacock's Gall* and *Nan Guan Cao*. *Qu Yuan* is the most famous historical play of its time. It presents a day in the life of the great poet Qu Yuan, showing his resolute spirit of patriotism and concern for the people, in impassioned scenes alternating with idyllic interludes. This artistic masterpiece created a sensation on its first performance and had a considerable impact at the time.

Mao Dun and his novel *Decay*. During the War Against Japan, Mao Dun wrote three novels, *Decay*, *Stories of the First Stage* and *Frosted Leaves Like February Flowers*, plus some non-fiction prose and translations. *Decay* is his best-known work of this period. A psychological story of a woman special agent of the Kuomintang in her progress from decadence to a new life, it exposes the blood-stained crimes of the Kuomintang's secret service. The detailed psychological analysis of the heroine's contradictory thoughts and feelings and the intricate plot gives this novel great artistic appeal.

(4) LITERATURE OF THE LATTER PERIOD OF THE WAR AGAINST JAPAN AND OF THE WAR OF LIBERATION (1942-1949)

The Yan'an Forum on Literature and Art and the Literary Rectification After the beginning of the War of Resistance Against Japan, large numbers of writers went to the base areas where they wrote many excellent works. But many people still did not recognize the importance of changing their world outlook to suit the new

---

[1] English translations of these plays forthcoming from FLP.

historical circumstances, so that certain mistaken ideas persisted and a wide ideological and emotional gap formed between writers and the worker and peasant masses. Reactionaries like Wang Shiwei in his articles "Wild Lilies" and "Politicians and Artists" made slanderous attacks on actual conditions in the base areas. As a consequence the Yan'an Forum on Literature and Art was convened in May 1942 to criticize Wang Shiwei's reactionary views and cleanse the muddled thinking in the literary world. In his famous "Talks at the Yan'an Forum on Literature and Art", Mao Zedong pointed out that literature is for the great masses of the people, primarily the workers, peasants and soldiers, and explained in Marxist terms the relationship between literature and politics and between literature and life. He also discussed a series of problems such as the critical inheritance of traditional literature, the relationship between popularization and raising standards in literature, and political and artistic criteria in literary criticism, and called on writers to go deeply into the life of the workers, peasants and soldiers to study from them and to reform their own outlook. The "Talks" have had a great significance in the development of revolutionary literature then and later. During the forum, the literary world carried out a literary rectification, uniting to criticize Wang Shiwei. After its conclusion, literary and art personnel went in groups to the front and to the villages, going among the great masses of workers, peasants and soldiers, and uniting with the masses of the people. Under the inspiration of the "Talks", literature took on a brand-new appearance within a few brief years, in the shape of an ever-increasing number of works on the new age, new characters and new subjects, written in popular, native Chinese forms.

Major Writers and Works in the Base Areas:

FICTION:

Zhao Shuli and *Rhymes of Li Youcai*. Zhao Shuli (1906-1970) developed a strong affection for folk literature from an early age, and his work as a village school teacher and other village activities made him very intimate with village life. When he began to write himself in 1931 he strove to give his work a popular, mass nature. In 1943 he published "The Marriage of Young Blacky",[1] a short story which established his name as a writer and was well received by the masses. It was followed by the short story "The Floor", the short novel, *Rhymes of Li Youcai*[2] and the novel, *Changes in Li Village*,[3] all on the theme of the reduction of land rent and interest rates in the liberated areas and the struggle against traitors and local despots. *Rhymes of Li Youcai* is one of the most outstanding work of the forties. Zhao Shuli's stories are simply and clearly related in witty, colloquial language, making him famous as a people's artist with a unique mass style. His stories have also had wide impact internationally.

Ding Ling and *The Sun Shines over the Sanggan River*. Ding Ling (b. 1907) established her name as a writer in the thirties with the short story "Diary of Miss Sophie" and the short novel *Water*. In 1946 she took

---

[1] English translation in *Rhymes of Li Youcai and Other Stories*, FLP, 1966.

[2] English translation published by FLP, 1966.

[3] English translation published by FLP, 1953.

part in the land reform movement and wrote *The Sun Shines over the Sanggan River*,[1] the first outstanding novel of the land reform movement in the history of modern Chinese literature. This novel won a Stalin Prize for Literature in 1951.

Zhou Libo and *The Hurricane*. In the thirties Zhou Libo (1908-1979) was an activist in the League of Left-Wing Writers, writing essays and literary criticism and translating foreign literature for a living. In 1946 he wrote his famous novel on land reform, *The Hurricane*.[2] The novel has a fresh flavour of the age and is rich in local colour. It won a Stalin Prize for Literature in 1951.

Other works from this period are *Uncle Gao*[3] by Ouyang Shan and *Sowing* by Liu Qing, two fine novels on village life in the liberated areas; *The Story of Ironbucket* by Ke Lan, *Heroes of the Lüliang Mountains* by Ma Feng and Xi Rong and *Daughters and Sons*[4] by Yuan Jing and Kong Que, a short novel and two full-length novels on the people's resistance in the liberated areas; and *The Moving Force*[5] by Cao Ming, a novel on industrial production in the liberated areas. The most outstanding short story was Sun Li's "Lotus Creek".[6]

POETRY:

Li Ji and *Wang Gui and Li Xiangxiang*. Li Ji (1922-1980) was familiar with the life and language of the people

---

[1] English translation published by FLP, 1954.
[2] English translation published by FLP, 1981.
[3] English translation published by FLP, 1957.
[4] English translation published by FLP, 1958.
[5] English translation published by the Culture Press, 1950.
[6] English translation published in *Lotus Creek and Other Stories* by FLP, 1982.

of north Shaanxi and the literary forms popular there. Using the north Shaanxi folk-song form known as *xintianyou* (literally, "free fight"), he wrote an excellent long narrative poem, *Wang Gui and Li Xiangxiang*[1] (1946) in praise of the struggle of the north Shaanxi people in building a new life. A skilful and moving depiction of a young peasant couple, it is one of the best poems in the history of modern Chinese literature.

Another excellent poem of the same period is "The Waters of the Zhanghe River" by Ruan Zhangjing (b. 1914). A song in praise of the emancipation of women, it relates the sufferings of the women in the Taihang Mountains under the barbaric oppression of traditional feudal customs, and warmly praises the liberation and new life achieved under the leadership of the Chinese Communist Party.

DRAMA:

A new opera, *The White-Haired Girl*. China's new opera has been formd by adding elements from traditional Chinese drama and Western opera to a foundation of northern Shaanxi *yangge*. *The White-Haired Girl*,[2] a collective creation of the Lu Xun Academy of the Arts scripted by He Jingzhi (b. 1924), a well-known poet, and Ding Yi (b. 1921), is the first major example of this form and a pioneering work in the development of new opera. In the tragedy of a poor young woman peasant, Xi'er, the opera exposes the cruelty of the landlord class and celebrates the victory of the peasants' struggle. It

---

[1] English translation published by FLP, 1978.
[2] English translation published by FLP, 1954.

has been translated and performed in many countries, and in 1951 it won a Stalin Prize for Literature. Afterwards, operas in the liberated areas made a great advance, with excellent works such as *Liu Hulan* (a collective composition by the Northwest War Dramatic Society), *River of Red Leaves* (by Ruan Zhangjing) and *Wang Xiuluan* (by Fu Duo).

The play, *Comrade, You Have Taken the Wrong Path*. Many new plays about workers, peasants and soldiers followed the publication of the "Talks", such as *Comrade, You Have Taken the Wrong Path*,[1] jointly written by Yao Zhongming and Chen Boer. It was the first play to depict leading cadres in the Communist Party and the Eighth Route Army, and to treat inner-Party struggles in the period of the War Against Japan. The characters are very lifelike and the dialogue is in the lively colloquial speech of the peasant masses. This play gives a new look to modern drama.

Other good plays of this time are *Set Your Vision Further* (a collective composition of the Central Hebei Frontline Dramatic Society, scripted by Hu Danfei), on the different attitude of two brothers on their sons who join the Eighth Route Army, *Grain* (a collective composition by Luo Ding, Zhang Fan and Zhu Xingnan), on the life and struggles behind enemy lines, and *Li Guorui* (by Du Feng), on life in the people's army.

Literary Works in the Kuomintang Areas In the areas under the control of the Kuomintang government, revolutionary literary personnel carried out a resolute struggle against the cultural dictatorship of the

---

[1] English translation published by FLP, 1962.

Kuomintang, and their resolute spirit was expressed in plays, satirical poetry and novels. The best-known plays of this period are Mao Dun's *Before and After the Qingming Festival,* Song Zhidi's *Foggy Chongqing* and Chen Baichen's satirical comedy, *A Picture of Promotion in Officialdom.* These plays are mostly exposures of the corruption of reactionary officials, and their depiction of the people's spirit of resistance played contributed towards boosting morale in the democratic movement of that time. Satirical poetry also flourished in the Kuomintang areas, the best-known work being Yuan Shuipai's *Ma Fantuo's Rustic Songs.* Zang Kejia published three volumes of political satire, *The Zero Degree of Life, Precious Baby* and *Winter.* In fiction, Huang Guliu's *The Story of Prawnball* had some impact. In three parts, it relates the adventures of the hero, Prawnball, in Hong Kong, the Kuomintang areas and the guerilla areas, ending with him taking the revolutionary path and becoming a hero.

4. CONTEMPORARY LITERATURE (1949-1981)

(1) BACKGROUND

The founding of the People's Republic of China was a major turning point in Chinese history. The Chinese revolution moved from the stage of new democracy to the stage of socialism, and Chinese literature moved accordingly into a new stage, the development of socialist literature. The literature of this period is known in China as *contemporary literature.*

Contemporary literature has developed on the basis of the revolutionary literature created since the May 4th Movement. In the course of the complex struggles which have taken place since then, China's revolutionary literary movement has accumulated rich experience and fostered a new generation of revolutionary writers, while Mao Zedong's "Talks at the Yan'an Forum on Literature and Art" determined the theoretical basis and orientation of proletarian literature. These conditions provided the necessary foundation for the formation and development of contemporary literature.

In July 1949, the two armies of revolutionary writers and artists, from the liberated areas and from the Kuomintang areas, joined forces in Beiping (present Beijing) to convene the first session of the First National Congress of Personnel in Literature and the Arts. The Congress established the orientation in literature and the arts for the new republic and founded a unified organization, the Chinese Federation of Writers and Artists. The separation that had existed between the two armies was thus brought to an end and a new course was set for the future.

In the period of national economic recovery and the First Five-Year Plan (1953-1957), the Chinese Communist Party and the people's government led the people to carry out reforms in society and politics, and a socialist transformation in economics. At the same time, they also initiated a series of campaigns against bourgeois idealism and feudal ideology in literature, and established a policy of encouraging literature and the arts with the slogans, "Let a hundred flowers blossom, weed through the old to bring forth the new" and "Let a hundred flowers blossom and a hundred schools of thought contend". Literary activities were carried out with vigour and vitality, and large numbers of literary personnel actively threw themselves into the mass struggle, familiarizing themselves with the new life and new people, and diligently creating works reflecting the great new age. The first fruits of the new literature had appeared by 1957. As many as 18,347 new works in literature and the arts were published in the period 1950-1957, and the number of literary and art periodicals expanded from over 40 in 1949 to 83. Among the widely read works of this period were the novels *Defend Yan'an* by Du Pengcheng, *A Thousand Miles of Lovely Land* by Yang Shuo and *Sanliwan Village* by Zhao Shuli, the plays *Dragon Beard Ditch* by Lao She and *The Long March* by Chen Qitong and the collection of essays *Who Are the Best Beloved?* by Wei Wei. Good beginnings were also made in the literature of ethnic minorities and children's literature. The number of members in the Chinese Writers' Association, a professional association of writers affiliated with the Federation of Writers and Artists, increased from 401 in 1949 to 708 in 1957 (not including members of local branches).

In the period from the fundamental completion of socialist reconstruction in 1956 up to the decade of the "cultural revolution", although the development of literature was affected by "Left" tendencies in political movements and literary criticism, there were still some conspicuous achievements. Many writers had accumulated and digested many years' experience, and a large number of excellent and important works in contemporary literature date from the late fifties and early sixties, such as the novels *Builders of a New Life* by Liu Qing, *Keep the Red Flag Flying* by Liang Bin, *Red Crag* by Luo Guangbin and Yang Yiyan, *The Song of Youth* by Yang Mo, *Tracks in the Snowy Forest* by Qu Bo and *Great Changes in a Mountain Village* by Zhou Libo; the plays *Teahouse* by Lao She, *Guan Hanqing* by Tian Han and *Cai Wenji* by Guo Moruo; the opera *The Red Guards of Honghu* and the song and dance epic *The East Is Red*. The appearance of these works marked the progress in maturity of Chinese socialist literature. In 1960, in the course of readjustments to the national economy by the Party and government, adjustments were also carried out in policies on literature and art. The Ministry of Culture and the Federation of Writers and Artists, on the basis of their past experience, put forward an eight-point agenda for reform in literature and the arts, and the situation gradually improved. Obvious progress was also made in regard to variety in subject-matter, styles and forms. The cinema and the theatre reached their highest standards since the founding of New China, and there were also notable achievements in lyrical essays and other nonfiction prose. Discussions were held on a series of questions in literary theory and criticism, such as the problem of subject-matter, historical plays, contradiction and conflict in drama and the question of readers' response in literature, and different views were exchanged. The number of members in the Chinese Writers' Association increased from 708 in 1957 to 1,059 in 1965. Improvements in the national economy encouraged the development of literature and the arts. Nevertheless, "Left" errors in the guiding ideology of work in literature had not been completely redressed, and due to the interference of Jiang Qing, Kang Sheng and their associates, mistaken and excessive political criticisms were made of certain literary works and views and also of some well-known figures in literary circles. The increasingly serious "Left" tendencies seriously affected the development of literature and presaged the imminent catastrophe.

When the "cultural revolution" began, literature and the arts were the first to come under attack from the Lin Biao and Jiang Qing counter-revolutionary cliques. During these 10 years, using the leadership powers in literature and the arts that they had usurped, they denied all the achievements in literature on groundless charges of "a black line in literature" and "revisionism". They proscribed many excellent Chinese and foreign works from the past and present, forced the dissolution of the Federation of Writers and Artists and its professional associations, and suspended publication of most of the literary periodicals. Many writers and artists were deprived of their right to practise their professions and were subjected to all kinds of persecution. However, the great majority of them remained firm, resolutely continuing to write or prepare material for future work.

After the smashing of the Jiang Qing counter-revolutionary clique in October 1976, writers and artists issued wide-ranging criticisms of the counter-revolutionary crimes of Lin Biao and Jiang Qing. The reputations of writers and artists who had suffered persecution and of works which had been wrongly criticized were restored, and the Federation of Writers and Artists and its professional associations were reactivated. The Party's correct policies on literature and the arts were restored and implemented, and socialist literature and art began to flourish anew. In 1979 the whole country entered a new age of socialist modernization. The Party Central Committee assumed the task of strengthening and improving Party leadership in literary activities, eliminating the pernicious vestiges of feudal ideology and bourgeois corruption. The Central Committee also emphasized the social obligations of writers and artists. The Fourth National Congress of Personnel in Literature and the Arts was convened in Beijing in November 1979. It carefully assessed the positive and negative experiences in literature and the arts over the previous 30 years and affirmed the tasks of literature and the arts in the new period. This meeting played an important role in stimulating the further development of literature and the arts. The four years between 1977 and 1980 was a fruitful time for literature. More than 300 novels, 520 short novels and 8,000 short stories were published, and substantial developments were also made in reportage literature, poetry, essays, children's literature, science writing and minority literature. Most of these works were rooted in real life, faithfully depicting the features of the age and the people's aspirations in a wide variety of forms and styles. They were of great value in leading people to a deeper understanding of reality, elevating their thinking and satisfying many different aesthetic needs. National awards were made for short stories, short novels, reportage literature, new poetry by middle-aged and young writers, children's literature and ethnic minority literature. Most of the award-winning works were on the new achievements in this period. Many of them represent considerable breakthroughs in ideology and art, greatly surpassing the standards set in the first 17 years of New China. There was also an unprecedented expansion in periodical publication. According to statistics for 1980, in that year there were 107 literary periodicals, more than 10 large-scale literary series and more than 70 periodicals in the arts. There was also a great increase in circulation. *People's Literature* and *Monthly Fiction,* the most important national literary periodicals, both printed over a million copies per issue, and most periodicals had a print run from 100,000 to 300,000 copies. Sustained efforts to encourage new talents resulted in large numbers of innovative and successful young and middle-aged writers joining the ranks of professional writers. In the last five years (1976-1981), 705 new members were admitted to the Chinese Writers' Association. At the national level the Association now has 1,550 members, of whom 70% are young or middle-aged. At the present time, writers and artists are being organized in different ways to go deeply into life and strengthen literary criticism, in order to improve their ideology and artistic training and sustain the healthy development of creative writing.

(2) MAJOR ACHIEVEMENTS IN CONTEMPORARY LITERATURE

Fiction The fiction of New China developed out of traditional Chinese fiction and progressive foreign fiction, on the foundation of the tradition of the May 4th Movement and in particular of the revolutionary realism developed since Mao Zedong's "Talks at the Yan'an Forum on Literature and Art", making new beginnings in subject-matter, characterization, themes and so on, and developing different artistic styles. Many works reached a fairly high level in ideology and art, symbolizing the great cause of new Chinese literature.

NOVELS:

Full-length novels occupy an important position in contemporary literature. The fifties began with the appearance of novels on the armed struggle of the previous years by writers who had personally taken part in the democratic revolution. The most famous of these are *Wall of Bronze* by Liu Qing,[1] *Stormy Years* by Sun Li,[2] *The Railway Guerrillas* by Zhi Xia,[3] and *Defend Yan'an!* by Du Pengcheng.[4] *Defend Yan'an!*, the most outstanding of this group, is an authentic coverage of the defence of Yan'an in the northeast campaign of 1947. It describes the revolutionary heroism of the officers and soldiers and has been praised as the first heroic epic of the people's revolutionary struggle since the founding of New China. The earliest novels on industrial subjects also appeared at this time, such as *The Iron Torrent* by Zhou Libo, *Coal Mines in May* by Xiao Jun and *Spring Comes to the Yalu River* (part one of *Latent Force*) by Lei Jia.

The latter half of the fifties saw the flowering of the novel. Many writers whose lives had been a long process of accumulation of experience and preparation introduced a broader range of subject-matter into the novel, and with it a level of ideology and art that was increasingly mature. Among the most outstanding were *Keep the Red Flag Flying* by Liang Bin,[5] *Builders of a New Life* by Liu Qing,[6] *The Song of Youth* by Yang Mo[7] and *Tracks in the Snowy Forest* by Qu Bo.[8] *Keep the Red Flag Flying* describes the sharp conflicts between

---

[1] English translation published by the FLP, 1954.
[2] English translation excerpted in *Chinese Literature*, 1963, 8.
[3] English translation published by FLP, 1966.
[4] English translation published by FLP, 1958.
[5] English translation published by FLP, 1980.
[6] English translation published by FLP, 1977.
[7] English translation published by FLP, 1978.
[8] English translation published by FLP, 1978.

two peasant families and the landlords in Suojing township on the plains of central Hebei in the thirties, praising the Party's leadership of the peasant movement and the militant spirit of the revolutionary peasants. Rich in national style and local colour, this novel is a magnificent epic of the peasant revolution in the thirties. *Builders of a New Life* depicts the process of socialist reform in village society through the changes in thinking, behaviour and psychology of characters from different classes and strata in a village on the plains of central Shaanxi during the cooperative movement. It describes the growth of a generation of new men and women, and creates genuinely realistic typical characters. *The Song of Youth* is an excellent novel on the student movement and revolutionary intellectuals of the thirties. The story moves swiftly and the finely drawn characters are authentic and moving. *Tracks in the Snowy Forest* is about the hardships and dangers faced by a detachment of the People's Liberation Army in the northeast in the early period of the War of Liberation as they wipe out a remnant bandit force. The unusual subject and the thrilling and complex plot are reminiscent of old Chinese tales of chivalry. Among other important novels of this period are *Great Changes in a Mountain Village* by Zhou Libo[1] and *Shoal of Golden Sand* by Yu Feng, on village life after Liberation; *Bitter Herbs* by Feng Deying[2] and *Militant Youth* by Xue Ke, on the complex struggles behind enemy lines; *Red Sun* by Wu Qiang,[3] on the battle of Menglianggu in Shandong during the War of Libera-

---

[1] English translation published by FLP, 1961.

[2] English translation excerpted in *Chinese Literature*, 1966, 4-6.

[3] English translation published by FLP, 1980.

tion; *Annals of a Provincial Town* by Gao Yunlan,[1] on the urban underground struggle and the patriotic struggles of the intellectuals; *Morning in Shanghai* by Zhou Erfu,[2] on the reform of the national bourgeoisie; *Three Family Lane* by Ouyang Shan,[3] on revolutionary history; *Steeled and Tempered* by Ai Wu[4] and *Braving Wind and Waves* by Cao Ming, on industry; *The Boundless Grasslands* by the Mongolian writer, Malqinhu, *The Joyful Golden Sand River* by the Yi writer, Li Qiao,[5] *We Sow the Seeds of Love* by Xu Huaizhong and *The Beautiful South* by the Zhuang writer, Lu Di, on the struggles of the minority peoples. These works describe different aspects of the vast picture of society and life in China over more than half a century of democratic revolution and socialist construction, and create a rich cast of characters, particularly working people as the masters of history. Writers also gradually developed their own distinctive styles.

After 1962, the development of "Left" errors in ideology and culture and the mistaken criticism of some literary works restricted the development of the novel. Despite this, some new novels made a considerable impact in the years between the beginning of the sixties and the eve of the "cultural revolution", such as *Red Crag* by Luo Guangbin and Yang Yiyan,[6] on the underground struggle

---

[1] English translation published by FLP, 1980.

[2] English translation of Volume I published by FLP, 1981.

[3] English translation excerpted in *Chinese Literature*, 1961, 5-6.

[4] English translation published by FLP, 1961.

[5] English translation of Volume I published as *Awakened Land* by FLP, 1962.

[6] English translation published by FLP, 1978.

in Chongqing on the eve of Liberation; *Li Zicheng*, Part I, by Yao Xueyin,[1] a historical novel on the peasant uprisings at the end of the Ming Dynasty; *Fragrant Seasons* by Chen Canyun, *Wind and Thunder* by Chen Dengke and *Bright Sunny Skies* by Hao Ran, on the cooperative movement in the countryside; and *Song of Ouyang Hai* by Jin Jingmai.[2] *Red Crag* had the widest circulation, attracting a broad range of readers because of its exciting plot, fresh characterization, sound construction and strong artistic appeal.

During the 10 years of the "cultural revolution", under extremely difficult circumstances, some literature was still produced which belonged to the people, such as *Li Zicheng*, Part II, by Yao Xueyin, *The Second Handshake* by Zhang Yang and *The Dagger* by Yang Peijin.[3] There were also several fairly good novels such as *The Mountains Turn Red* by Li Ruqing, *Bright Red Star* by Li Xintian,[4] *Yesterday's Battle* by Meng Weizai, *Tale of the Big Knife* by Guo Chengqing, *The Tumultuous Mountains and Seas* by Qu Bo and *Swift Spring Tides* by Ke Fei.

The novel began to flourish again after 1976. The most outstanding of recent works are Wei Wei's *The East* and Yao Xueyin's *Li Zicheng*. *The East* is about the War to Resist America and Aid Korea; it describes fierce battles and also portrays the ideological struggles within the army. The heroes are authentically depicted in their progress towards maturity with all their inner conflicts,

---

[1] English translation excerpted in *Chinese Literature, 1978*, 4-8.

[2] English translation published by FLP, 1966.

[3] English translation published by FLP, 1979.

[4] English translation published by FLP, 1974.

so that they become people of flesh and blood whom we can love and respect. *Li Zicheng* is a masterpiece of the historical novel; Parts I and II have already been published and a further three parts are planned. The novel praises the historic achievements of the peasant's revolutionary wars and gives a broad picture of life in society and the class struggle in the mid-17th century, reaching a high standard in both ideology and art. *Xu Mao and His Daughters*,[1] a novel on life in a Sichuan village by Zhou Keqin, is one of the best recent novels on the countryside. Other novels which have had some impact include *The Story of Emancipation* by Liang Bin, *The Yellow River Runs East* by Li Zhun, *Warm Are the Steep Cliffs* by Gao Ying, *The Scarlet Dragon and Crimson Phoenix* by Chen Dengke, *Mountain Chrysanthemum* by Feng Deying, *Morning in Shanghai*, Part III, by Zhou Erfu, *Dawn in the East* by Yang Mo and *Road to Life* by Zhu Lin, a young woman writer. Two new novels by older writers, *In Days of Bitter Cold* by Ding Ling and *Bright Flowers and Dark Willows* by Ouyang Shan are now being serialized. *Dawn* by the Tibetan writer Yixi Choma has also won acclaim.

SHORT NOVELS:

Not many short novels were published in the 17 years before the "cultural revolution", but there were a few excellent works such as *Living Hell* by Chen Dengke,[2] on the cruel oppression and exploitation practised by the

---

[1] English translation excerpted in *Chinese Literature*, 1981, 5-6.

[2] English translation published by FLP, 1955.

landlords and reactionaries, and the people's resistance to them; *Unfading Flowers* by Ma Jia,[1] on a cadre troop's encounters with the enemy on the advance into the northeast after victory in the War of Resistance; *A Thousand Miles of Lovely Land* by Yang Shuo,[2] on the War to Resist America and Aid Korea; *The Blacksmith and the Carpenter* by Sun Li[3] and *We Crossed the Bridge Together* by Liu Shude[4] on life in the countryside and the cooperative movement.

After 1976, the short novel entered its most flourishing period, attracting considerable attention with its achievements. In the last four years (1977-1981) more than 300 short novels have been published, including more than 170 in 1980 alone. This is an unprecedented development in the history of Chinese literature since the May 4th Movement. Apart from a few works on revolutionary history, such as *Women Soldiers Rejoin Their Unit* by Deng Youmei, *Peony* by Xu Chi and *Catkin Willow Flats*[5] by Liu Shaotang, the majority are about present-day life. *It Is Always Spring* by Chen Rong, *Uncharted River* by Ye Weilin, *Flower-Strewn Crossroads* by Feng Jicai, *The Butterfly* by Wang Meng,[6] *Spring in Hiding* by Cen Sang and *The Daughter's Letter* by Qin Zhaoyang depict different aspects of the sufferings and struggles of various kinds of people such as cadres, intellectuals and the young in the chaotic years of the "cultural revolution". *A Tale*

---

[1] English translation published by FLP, 1961.
[2] English translation published by FLP, 1979.
[3] English translation in *Chinese Literature*, 1961, 7.
[4] English translation published by FLP, 1963.
[5] Partial English translation in *Chinese Literature*, 1982, 5.
[6] English translation in *Chinese Literature*, 1981, 1.

of Tianyun Mountain by Lu Yanzhou describes the struggle around the reversal of incorrect verdicts on people, while *At Middle Age* by Chen Rong,[1] *Ah!* by Feng Jicai, *Spring Chill* by Wang Xiyan and *The Trailblazers* by Jiang Zilong depict the complex conflicts in real life at the present time. The 15 works which received the *People's Literature* Awards for the best short novels of 1977-1980 were popularly acclaimed as the best works to emerge in recent years, and collectively reflect the achievements of the short novel in this period.

SHORT STORIES:

Vast numbers of short stories have appeared since 1949. Many of them have reached a quite high level in ideology and art, and many artistically mature writers have emerged with their own distinctive styles. The most fertile periods for the short story were the mid-fifties, the early sixties and the new period after 1976.

The most outstanding achievements of the short story before the "cultural revolution" were the works depicting the struggles during the democratic revolution and life in the countryside. "Membership Dues" by Wang Yuanjian,[2] "Dawn on the River" by Jun Qing,[3] "The March Snow Flower" by Xiao Ping,[4] "Mama's Story" by Han Zi, "Long

---

[1] English translation in *Chinese Literature*, 1980, 10.

[2] English translation in *Dawn and on the River and Other Stories*, FLP, 1957.

[3] English translation in *Chinese Literature*, 1978, 8 and in *Dawn on the River*, FLP, 1957.

[4] English translation in *Chinese Literature*, 1957, 4 and *The Young Coal Miner and Other Stories*, FLP, 1958.

Flows the Stream" by Liu Zhen,[1] and "The Lilies" by Ru Zhijuan,[2] depict different aspects of the people's struggles and heroic deeds during the democratic revolution. Sha Ting, Zhou Libo, Zhao Shuli, Ma Feng, Xi Rong, Wang Wenshi, Kang Zhuo and Li Zhun concentrated on stories about life in the countryside, with excellent results. Fine works such as "The Story of Li Shuangshuang" by Li Zhun,[3] "Wind and Waves" by Sha Ting, "My First Superior" by Ma Feng,[4] "The Night of the Snowstorm" by Wang Wenshi,[5] "Spring Sowing, Autumn Harvest" by Kang Zhuo[6] and "A Visitor from Beijing" and "The Family on the Other Side of the Mountain" by Zhou Libo[7] depict the conflicts and new life in the cooperative movement in the countryside. Works such as "I Knew All Along" by Ma Feng,[8] "Characters of Steel" by Zhao Shuli and "Sister Lai" by Xi Rong mainly focus in a realistic and perceptive way on the mentality of small private holders and their clashes with collectivism.

The treatment of workers' life in the first 17 years after Liberation is a rather weak area, but there are a few

---

[1] English translation in *Chinese Literature*, 1963, 2 and *Wild Bull Village — Chinese Short Stories*, FLP, 1965.

[2] English translation in *Chinese Literature*, 1959, 2 and *I Knew All Along and Other Stories*, FLP, 1960.

[3] English translation in *Chinese Literature*, 1960, 6.

[4] English translation in *Chinese Literature*, 1981, 9 and in *The Sun Has Risen*. FLP, 1961.

[5] English translation in *Dawn on the River and Other Stories*, FLP, Beijing, 1957 and *The Night of the Snowstorm*, FLP, 1979.

[6] English translation in *When the Sun Comes Up*, FLP, 1961.

[7] English translation of the latter in *Chinese Literature*, 1960, 2 and in *Sowing the Clouds*, FLP, 1961.

[8] English translation in *Chinese Literature*, 1959, 7, *I Knew All Along and Other Stories*. FLP, 1960 and *The Sun Has Risen*, FLP, 1961.

excellent stories such as "A New Home"[1] and "Return by Night" by Ai Wu, and "Yan'an People"[2] and "Night at the Worksite" by Du Pengcheng, which describe the construction of the northwest railways. Apart from these, some writers of worker origin have written works which have found a strong welcome among the masses, such as "Man of Special Cut"[3] and "Who Are the Creators of Miracles?" by Hu Wanchun, "The Seeds" by Tang Kexin, "One Short Year" by Fei Liwen[4] and "The S.S. International Friendship" by Lu Junchao.[5] Excellent stories from the early sixties are "The Road Test" by Zhang Tianming,[6] "Line Patrol" by Liu Anqi and "Fighting the Ice" by Xiao Yuxuan.[7]

Stories about army life, on themes like battle training, the relationship between the army and the people and the relationship between officers and soldiers, such as "Wind Bucker" by Ren Binwu,[8] "Fifty-Metre Limit" by Lin Yu and "Shipwreck Reef" by Qi Ping, along with stories on the lives of minority ethnic groups such as *More Southern Journeys* by Ai Wu[9] and "Daji and Her Father"

---

[1] English translation in *A New Home and Other Stories*, FLP, 1955.

[2] English translation in *I Knew All Along and Other Stories*, FLP, 1960.

[3] English translation in *Man of a Special Cut*, FLP, 1963.

[4] English translation in *Homeward Journey and Other Stories*, FLP, 1957.

[5] English translation in *Chinese Literature*, 1959, 6 and *A Snowy Day and Other Stories*, FLP, 1960.

[6] English translation in *Chinese Literature*, 1963, 7.

[7] English translation in *Chinese Literature*, 1964, 6.

[8] English translation in *Chinese Literature*, 1966, 2.

[9] English translation in *Wild Bull Village*, FLP, 1965.

by Gao Ying, also received favourable comment from readers in this period.

In the lively atmosphere created in 1956 by the policy of "letting a hundred flowers blossom and a hundred schools of thought contend", some young writers published stories touching on the negative, dark sides of life, such as "The Young Newcomer in the Organization Department" by Wang Meng, "Sunset over the Fields" by Liu Shaotang, "Dark Sails" by Li Zhun, "Silence" by Qin Zhaoyang, and "The Inside Story of Our Paper" and "At the Bridge Site" by Liu Binyan. Their criticism of bureaucratism and doctrinairism was of educational significance at that time. However, these stories and even their authors were wrongly criticized in the anti-Rightist struggle of 1957. They have now been republished under the title *A Second Blooming*.

After 1976, short stories led the way in breaking through the mould set by Jiang Qing and her associates, opening up hitherto forbidden areas and extending the range of subject-matter. A stream of new authors and new works contributed to the unprecedented flourishing of the short story at this time. Eighty stories were chosen in polls conducted by the editorial board of *People's Literature* in 1979, 1980 and 1981 to select the best short stories from all over the country, and collectively reflect the high level of short story writing in recent years.

These 80 short stories break new ground in theme, subject-matter and characterization. Many of them are about the serious disasters suffered by people through Lin Biao, Jiang Qing and their associates and also the people's resistance to them, such as "The Teacher" by Liu

Xinwu,[1] "The Scar" (also known as "The Wound") by Lu Xinhua[2] and "Sacred Duty" by Wang Yaping.[3] Some go even further, dealing with the dangers created by "Left" errors in work and historical lessons, such as "A Story Out of Sequence" by Ru Zhijuan,[4] "Reminiscence" by Zhang Xian and "Li Shunda Builds a House" by Gao Xiaosheng. There are also stories on the complex contradictions in this new period in history, which expose bureaucratism, the "special privileges" mentality and rigid thinking, and stories about young people's lives, such as "Thirty Million Yuan" by Ke Yunlu,[5] and "The Barber's Tale" and "A Spate of Visitors" by Wang Meng.[6] Because they start from real life, bring out social problems of deep concern to people and point out current errors, these stories are read with deep concern. In 1980-1981, there has been a distinct increase in stories on the arduous efforts and heroic sacrifices made for the sake of realizing the four modernizations in agriculture, industry, science and national defence, such as "Manager Qiao Assumes Office" by Jiang Zilong,[7] "Anecdote from the Western Line" by Xu Huaizhong and "A Soldier in the

---

[1] English translation in *Chinese Literature*, 1979, 1 and *Prize-Winning Stories from China, 1978-1979*, FLP, 1981.

[2] English translation in *Chinese Literature*, 1979, 3 and *Prize-Winning Stories from China, 1978-1979*.

[3] English translation in *Chinese Literature*, 1979, 6 and *Prize-Winning Stories from China, 1978-1979*.

[4] English translation in *Prize-Winning Stories from China, 1978-1979*.

[5] English translation in *Chinese Literature*, 1981, 8.

[6] English translation of both in *Chinese Literature*, 1980, 7.

[7] English translation in *Chinese Literature*, 1980, 2 and *Prize-Winning Stories from China, 1978-1979*.

Tianshan Mountains" by Li Binkui.[1] A significant theme is the patriotism of intellectuals in stories such as "Body and Soul" by Zhang Xianliang and "The Empty Nest" by Bing Xin. The images of new men and women of socialism created in these works are inspiring and compelling.

There have also been new experiments in form and style in the short story. Among the most innovative writers is Wang Meng, who has broken up the traditional structure of plot and composition, critically assimilating the Western technique of "stream of consciousness".

Poetry Chinese poetry written today falls into two groups, "new" poetry which is based on new forms introduced during the May 4th Movement and is written in the modern spoken language, and "old" poetry which is based on traditional Chinese poetic forms and is written in the old literary language. The great bulk of poetry written since 1949 has been in the new style.

The early fifties was a flourishing period for new poetry. The birth of New China and the great changes in social life greatly stimulated the older poets to find new ways to depict the new life, while a stream of new young writers supplied a fresh vitality. It was a time of many poets and many poems. The content and themes of these poems were comparatively concentrated, most of them being in praise of New China and the new life. Among the excellent poems of this kind were Guo Moruo's "Ode to New China", Ke Zhongping's "Hold High Our Five-Starred Flag", He Qifang's "Our Greatest Festive Day", Wang Xin's "Song of Our Land" and Zang Kejia's "Some People", but the greatest impact was made by He Jing-

---

[1] English translation in *Chinese Literature*, 1981, 8.

zhi's "Singing Aloud" and Guo Xiaochuan's "Plunging into the Fiery Struggle" and "Advancing Through Difficulties". He Jingzhi's poem describes in fresh, imaginative language the great achievements in new Chinese life, reflecting the feelings of joy and confidence of the broad masses towards their new life and expressing the sincere love and high trust that they have for the Party. Guo Xiaochuan's poems boldly and earnestly issue an enthusiastic summons to youth to create a new life. The publication of these poems aroused a great response among the masses, especially among the young. Another important theme of this period was the fiery struggle on the construction battlefront, praising selfless toil and revolutionary heroism. Poems on this theme which made an impact include Li Ji's *Songs from the Yumen Oilfields*,[1] on the petroleum workers of the northwest, Shao Yanxiang's "Going to Distant Places", Gong Liu's "In the North", Wen Qie's "Tianshan Pastorals", Tian Jian's "Songs for the Horsehead Fiddle" and Gu Gong's "At the Foot of the Himalayas". There were also many poems in defence of peace and the poet's homeland, such as Shi Fangyu's "The Mightiest Voice of Peace", a battle song opposing wars of aggression and in defence of world peace, Wei Yang's "Give Me the Gun!" and "My Country I Return to Thee", on the War to Resist America and Aid Korea, and Ai Qing's "The Atlantic", on the international struggle.

The "hundred flowers" policy of 1956 gave a great stimulus to poetry. The range of subject-matter became broader, bringing in poems that depicted internal contradictions among the people and pointed out current errors,

---

[1] English translation published by FLP, 1957.

such as Ai Qing's "The Gardener's Dream" and Liu Shahe's "Plants". Nature poems, love poems, fables and satiric poems also appeared at this time. A greater variety of forms, such as free verse, regulated poetry, folk song, and even old poetry, developed freely. However, in the extension of the anti-Rightist struggle of 1957 some poems and poets were wrongly criticized, causing a setback to the development of new poetry.

In 1958 there was a nationwide movement to collect and create new folk songs, and a great number of new folk song collections were published. An anthology of 300 folk songs compiled by Guo Moruo and Zhou Yang under the title *Songs of the Red Flag*[1] was published in 1959. Some of the folk songs in this collection are spirited and moving, but under the influence of current Leftist ideology, many are exaggerated, glossing over the truth and violating the reality of life.

Following the adjustments to literary policies in the early sixties, poetry flourished anew. Some of the political lyrics of this time were quite mature ideologically and artistically. They reflected the major questions of the time, expressing the firm will of the Chinese people in despising and conquering difficulties and their devotion to the liberation of all mankind. Among these works are He Jingzhi's "Song of Lei Feng", Guo Xiaochuan's "Green Gauze Tent", Ruan Zhangjing's "Advancing with 'The Internationale' on Our Lips", Yan Zhen's "Bamboo Spears", Lu Qi's "Willow Village Revisited", Zhang Zhimin's "The Contest Platform", Sha Bai's "The Great River Flows East"[2] and Liang Shangquan's "The Highlands in

---

[1] Abridged English translation published by FLP, 1961.
[2] English translation in *Chinese Literature*, 1965, 8.

Ferment". However, there was not much variety in subject-matter, style or form, and the ideas tended to be vague and general.

Excellent long narrative poems appeared in the fifties, such as Qiao Lin's "Michelia", Li Ji's "The Story of Yang Gao", Guo Xiaochuan's "In Praise of the White Snow" and "Deep Mountain Valleys", Li Bing's "Zhao Qiao'er", Liang Shangquan's "Red Cloud Cliff", and "The Cloak of a Hundred Feathers" by the Zhuang poet Wei Qilin.[1] A further development took place in the sixties, as well-known poems like Wen Qie's *Flames of Vengeance*,[2] Guo Xiaochuan's "Trilogy of the General" and Wang Zhiyuan's "Hutao Slope" skilfully blended narrative with lyricism. Narrative poems from minority ethnic groups are the precious distillation of their collective wisdom; well known examples published at this time are "King Gesar", a heroic epic from Tibet, "Gada Meilin", on modern Mongolian life, and "Zhaoshu Village", a love poem from the Dai people of Yunnan. The best of these in terms of artistic achievement and impact is *Ashima*,[3] from the Yi people of Yunnan, which shows their love of work and freedom and their struggle for freedom of choice in marriage.

During the decade of the "cultural revolution", many upright poets were persecuted because of their writings. It was under these difficult conditions that Guo Xiaochuan wrote poems like "Autumn in Tuanbowa" and "Autumn Song".[4] In April 1976 around the time of the

---

[1] English translation in *Chinese Literature*, 1962, 8.
[2] Excerpted in English translation in *Chinese Literature*, 1961, 5 & 12.
[3] English translation published by FLP, 1981.
[4] Both in *Chinese Literature*, 1977, 5-6.

Qingming Festival, a sea of poems appeared in Tiananmen Square: using poetry as their weapon, the broad masses angrily denounced the Jiang Qing counter-revolutionary clique and commemorated Zhou Enlai, writing a splendid page in the history of poetry. After 1976 several volumes of these poems were officially published under the title *The Tiananmen Poems*[1] to the great joy of the broad masses.

In the last five years (1976-1981), poetry has flourished once more. A great number of recent poems praise the people's great victory, mercilessly castigate the crimes of Lin Biao, Jiang Qing and their associates, and commemorate and praise Zhou Enlai and other veteran revolutionaries. Excellent works include Li Ying's "Grief in January",[2] Ke Yan's "Where Are You, Premier Zhou?", He Jingzhi's "October in China" and Liu Zhen's prose poem, "We Weep for you, Commander Peng Dehuai".

In recent years, poets have written after deep reflection thoughtful and exploratory poems on the four modernizations, human ideals, youth, and various problems in real life. Poems such as Ai Qing's "In Praise of Light" and "On the Crest of a Wave", Shao Yanxiang's "Chinese Cars Roar Down the Expressways", Bai Hua's "Sun, No One Can Monopolize You", Gong Liu's "Stars", Liu Shahe's "Weeping", Luo Gengye's "Dissatisfied", Qu Youyuan's "Meetings Where People Snore" and Shu Ting's "My Motherland, Dear Motherland"[3] have aroused a strong response from the masses.

---

[1] English translation published by FLP, 1979.
[2] Abridged English translation in *Chinese Literature*, 1979, 9.
[3] English translation in *Chinese Literature*, 1980, 10.

Old-style poetry in New China has successfully depicted modern life and expressed revolutionary feelings. Mao Zedong's old poems have had the greatest impact. The 43 poems by Mao Zedong published between 1957 and 1978 (most of them written before 1949) illustrate a revolutionary career that spanned half a century. Along with their important ideological message, the poems also have great artistic appeal, showing the author's remarkable skill at handling the strict requirements of old poetry. Many other members of the same generation of proletarian revolutionaries, such as Chen Yi, Zhou Enlai, Dong Biwu, Zhu De, Ye Jianying and Tao Zhu also wrote old poems to a greater or lesser extent, making a splendid contribution to contemporary Chinese poetry. Others like Guo Moruo and Zhao Puchu have written many new poems in various old styles which capture the spirit of the new age and are greatly appreciated by readers.

Non-Fictional Prose Non-fictional prose, like poetry, is one of the earliest literary forms to appear in China, and the past few thousand years have produced many great prose writers and imperishable works. After Liberation in 1949, the new life and society created a new realm for literary prose. Among the varieties of prose which have flourished since 1949, excellent works have been produced in the following categories: reportage, news stories and feature articles; personal or lyrical essays and travel sketches; biographies and memoirs.

REPORTAGE, NEWS STORIES AND FEATURE ARTICLES:

Great achievements were made in news story and feature writing in the early fifties and sixties. During the War to Resist America and Aid Korea in the early fifties, writers went to the front lines and produced a large amount of news stories and special features depicting the heroic deeds of the volunteer officers and soldiers and their patriotic, internationalist spirit. The works with the greatest impact were "Who Are the Best Beloved?" and "A Reluctant Parting" by Wei Wei, "We Meet Commander Peng Dehuai" and "Living Among Heroes" by Ba Jin[1] "Korea Marches On" and "A Vow for Peace" by Liu Baiyu, "On the Banks of the Chongchon-gang" by Hua Shan and "I Come from Sangkumryung" by Han Zi. In the mid-fifties, the focus shifted to depicting China's large-scale economic construction and praising the working people's arduous toil. Excellent examples of this kind of reportage are "The Age of Fairy Tales" by Hua Shan, "Chairman Mao Laughs at the Yellow River" by Zang Kejia, "Sketches from the Qaidam Basin" by Li Ruobing,[2] "Going to Fuziling" by Qin Yi and "This Generation of Ours" by Xu Chi. Among the better essays of the late fifties are "From Hulan Ergi to Qiqihar" by Liu Baiyu,[3] "Precious Land, Precious Man, Precious Thing" by Wei Gangyan, "Snowflakes Flying at Qilian" by Li Ruobing, "Night Journey Through Lingguan Gorge" by Du Pengcheng and "On the Bank of the Pearl River" by Chen Canyun. Ideologically and artistically mature works of the early sixties include "A Model County Party Secretary — Jiao Yulu" by Mu Qing and others, "Chairman Mao's Good Fighter — Lei Feng" by

---

[1] English translation in *Living Among Heroes,* FLP, 1954.
[2] English translation in *Chinese Literature,* 1960, 2.
[3] English translation in *Chinese Literature,* 1958, 6.

Tong Xiwen, "How Does a Red Peach Bloom" by Wei Gangyan, "Korea — Land of the Morning Sun" by Huang Gang, "The Slavey Shoulders the Red Flag" by Huang Zongying, "Hands" by Ba Jin and others, and "At the Foot of Mount Qilian" by Xu Chi. These works played an important educational role among the broad masses.

After 1976, reportage was the first form of prose writing to be revived, making a breakthrough both in the breadth and depth of its depiction of life and society. The main subject-matter of reportage literature in recent years has been the accomplishments of intellectuals and scientists and great events in society. The first to open up this hitherto forbidden ground was Xu Chi's "The Goldbach Conjecture",[1] a realistic narrative of the frustrating experiences of the mathematician Chen Jingrun and his dedication to science. Other reports on scientists followed in its wake, such as "A New Resurgence on the Asian Continent" by Huang Gang, "The Tree of Life Is Evergreen" by Xu Chi, "The Flight of the Wild Geese" by Huang Zongying[2] and "How Many Children She Has" by Li You. In addition, "In Praise of Middle Age" and "With Head High, I Draw My Sword" by Li You, "In Trust for Premier Zhou" by Mu Qing and others, "Recalling the Iron Man" by Wei Gangyan, "The Skipper" and "The Pursuer of Beauty" by Ke Yan, "The Caged Eagle's Will" by Li Lingxiu, "There Are a Hundred Thousand Fiery Hearts Here" by Li Rui, "Vigorous Efforts for a Prosperous Land" by Cheng Shuzhen, "A Warm Current" by Zhang Qie and "The Country Above All" by Chen Zufen depict a wide range of characters from all levels of society, such as athletes, workers, peasants, artists,

---

[1] English translation in *Chinese Literature,* 1978, 11.
[2] English translation in *Chinese Literature,* 1981, 10.

cadres and boat captains, portraying with great artistic skill their unflagging perseverance in their country's service and the vicissitudes of their lives. At the time of the counter-offensive against Vietnam, many writers went to the front and wrote reports praising the border soldiers' heroic spirit and lofty sentiments: "From the Precipice to the Level Path" by Lei Duo and "Ode to Love" by Ai Pu and others are excellent examples.

LYRICAL ESSAYS:

The personal or lyrical essay has a very long tradition in China, and its progress since the founding of New China has also been very great. Good work by writers who specialize in this type of essay includes "Red Leaves on Xiangshan" by Yang Shuo,[1] "Notes on Huangshan" by Han Zi, "Feelings at the Altar to Land and Grain" by Qin Mu, "A Trip to Tianshan" by Bi Ye,[2] "Her Second Chance" by He Wei,[3] "Leaf Whistle" by Guo Feng and "The Sound of Flute at Dawn" by Ke Lan. Well-known essays by older writers include "Remembering Lu Xun" and "Autumn Night" by Ba Jin, "The Small Tangerine Lamp" by Bing Xin and "A Trip Over Three Lakes" by Ye Shengtao. The early sixties was a golden age in the development of the essay, which took many different forms from travel notes to random jottings. The essayists' mastery of artistic style also became increasingly mature. Well-known works of this period include "Three Days on the Changjiang",[1] "Notes on Cherry Blossom"

---

[1] English translation in *A Selection of Prose Pieces*, FLP, 1980.
[2] English translation in *Chinese Literature*, 1957, 3.
[3] English translation in *Mirages and Sea-Markets*, FLP, 1962.

and "Short Notes of Pingming" by Liu Baiyu, "Snowy Waves", "Litchi Honey" and "Ode to the Camellia" by Yang Shuo[2] and "Flower City" and "The Earth" by Qin Mu. There were also essays recalling the years of arduous struggle, such as "Recalling Those Years, Trifling Matters Such as Clothing Should Not Be Treated Lightly" by Cao Jinghua and "A Spinning Wheel", "Notes on a Garden" and "Song" by Wu Boxiao.

In the last few years, the lyrical essay has gradually been revived. Excellent works have appeared commemorating senior revolutionaries, such as "Chang'an Avenue in October" by Yuan Ying, "March in Southern Anhui" and "The Poetic Quality of Meiling" by Han Zi, "The Towering Taihang Mountains" by Liu Baiyu, "My Visits to the Riverside Pavilion" by He Wei,[3] "A Letter" by Ba Jin, "A Letter That Was Finally Sent" by Tao Siliang and "Sunrise at the Sacred Fountain" by Li Ruobing.

BIOGRAPHIES AND REMINISCENCES:

During the long years of the new-democratic and socialist revolutionaries in China, millions of Communist Party members, heroes, models and ordinary soldiers devoted their lives to the struggle for the people's benefit. It was the glorious task of Chinese literature to write their biographies and record their heroic deeds, to pass on their revolutionary spirit to future generations. The earliest biographical literature after the founding of New China was *Stories of the Chinese People's Volunteers*, a record of

---

[1] English translation in *Mirages and Sea-Markets*, FLP, 1962.
[2] English translations in *A Selection of Prose Pieces*, FLP, 1980.
[3] English translation in *Chinese Literature*, 1977, 4.

the great achievements of the People's Volunteer Army compiled not long after the end of the war in Korea. In 1956, the General Political Department of the Chinese People's Liberation Army solicited contributions for "Thirty Years of the Chinese People's Liberation Army", a series of memoirs under the title *A Single Spark Can Start a Prairie Fire*.[1] In 1957 the Chinese Youth Press published a collection called *The Red Flag Flutters*, consisting of biographies and reminiscences. Since the founding of New China, published biographies and reminiscences have run into millions of words, the collections mentioned above having the greatest impact.

Other important works include *Son of the Working Class* by Wu Yunduo,[2] *Mama Xia, a Revolutionary Mother* by Huang Gang, *My Family* by Tao Cheng,[3] *Reminiscences of the Long March* by Cheng Fangwu, *Recollections of He Long* by Sha Ting, *Eternal Life in the Flames* by Luo Guangbin, *Iron Bars But Not a Cage — Wang Ruofei's Days in Prison* by Yang Zhiling,[4] *On the Long March with Chairman Mao* by Chen Changfeng,[5] *Eleven Years with Vice-Chairman Zhou* by Long Feihu and *By the Side of Commander Peng* by Jing Xizhen.

Children's Literature Since the founding of New China, children's literature has received great attention and positive support from the Chinese government. As early as 1953, the First National Children's Literature Award was held to encourage the writing of children's

---

[1] Excerpts in English translation in *Chinese Literature*, 1959, 2 and 1960, 7 and in *The Unquenchable Spark*, FLP, 1964.

[2] English translation published by FLP, 1956.

[3] English translation published by FLP, 1960.

[4] English translation published by FLP, 1962.

[5] English translation published by FLP, 1972.

literature. In 1955, Beijing and Shanghai established presses specializing in children's literature which edited and published many excellent works, including poems, fairy tales, novels, stories, plays, magazines and newspapers. After 1976, the Chinese Writers' Association and the departments responsible for children's publications convened a series of meetings on problems in writing and publishing children's literature. In 1979 the departments concerned jointly sponsored the Second National Children's Literature Award in which 212 works published between 1954 and 1979 were commended. At the same time, to commemorate the 30th anniversary of the founding of New China, the People's Literature Press published several anthologies of children's literature, covering almost 800 excellent works from the past 30 years and containing more than two million words. In 1981, the State Publications Bureau established an award fund for children's reading materials, and two more presses specializing in children's literature were established, one in Tianjin and one in Sichuan; the People's Press in each province also set up an editorial department for children's reading materials; and the number of periodicals in children's literature increased from three in 1979 to 11. Children's literature is now in a flourishing state of development.

Since 1949, the ranks of writers for children have steadily expanded. They include older writers who have devoted themselves to writing children's literature since the thirties or forties, such as Ye Shengtao, Bing Xin, Gao Shiqi, Zhang Tianyi, Yan Wenjing, Chen Bochui, He Yi, Ye Junjian, Bao Lei and Jin Jin. New and talented writers who emerged in the fifties include Liu Zhen, Ke Yan, Gao Xiangzhen, Ren Dalin, Xu Guangyao, Liu

Houming, Ren Deyao, Lin Lan, Xiao Ping, Zhang Youde, Ren Daxing and Ren Rongrong. In addition, a fresh new force has entered the field in the last few years, bringing keen and original new thinking to children's literature. Many famous writers have also written good works for children, such as Guo Moruo, Ba Jin, Wei Jinzhi, Jin Yi, Zhou Erfu, Zhou Libo, Ma Feng, Kang Zhuo, Yang Shuo, Yuan Jing, Wei Wei, Zhi Xia, Tian Jian, Li Ji, Ruan Zhangjing, Yuan Ying and He Jingzhi, adding new treasures to the storehouse of children's literature.

FAIRY TALES:

Fairy tales are the earliest form of children's literature to appear in China. The full-length fairy story *The Magic Gourd* by Zhang Tianyi[1] and *Next-Time Port* by Yan Wenjing,[2] both from the fifties, have great educational value and are wonderfully imaginative; both have been translated into many foreign languages. Other works popular among children are *Tales Brought by the Spring Breeze* by Jin Jin, *The Magic Brush* by Hong Xuntao, *Wild Grapes* by Ge Cuilin, *The Curious Red Star* by Huang Qingyun and *The Adventures of a Little Rag Doll* by Sun Youjun.[3] More recent works include *The Little Shell in the Waves* by Sun Youjun, *The Little Pony and the Little Donkey* by Yang Shuan, *Nu Nu, the Little Elephant* by Kang Fumin and *The Adventures of Little Fofo* by Sun Youchen.

---

[1] English translation published by FLP, 1971.
[2] English translation published by FLP, 1958.
[3] English translation published by FLP, 1980.

POEMS:

Well-known poems include *The Golden Sea Shell* by Ruan Zhangjing,[1] *The Story of the Little Soldier* by Ke Yan, *Liu Wenxue* by Yuan Ying, *Guess What My Father's Job Is* by Ren Rongrong and *My Secret* by Bing Xin. More recent works are *Xingxing and I on the Telephone* by Zhang Qiusheng and *The Sky's Song* by Liu Bin.

PLAYS:

The Big Grey Wolf by Zhang Tianyi,[2] *Magic Aster* by Ren Deyao,[3] *The Geese Fly in Formation* by Liu Houming and *The Newspaper Boy,* jointly written by Shao Chongfei, Wei You, Wang Zheng and Lin Kehuan, have all had some impact. More recent work popular among children includes *The Strange 101* by Luo Ying, Pan Yaobin and Cheng Shiru, and *The Teacher* by Ouyang Yibing.

FICTION:

Well-known novels and short story collections include *How Luo Wenying Became a Pioneer* by Zhang Tianyi,[4] *Snowflakes* by Yang Shuo,[5] *Good Mother* and *Little Rong and I* by Liu Zhen, *Little Soldier Zhang Gazi* by Xu

---

[1] English translation published by FLP, 1961.
[2] English translation published by FLP, 1965.
[3] English translation published by FLP, 1966.
[4] English translation in *Chinese Literature,* 1954, 3 and published by FLP, 1954.
[5] English translation published by FLP, 1979.

Guangyao,[1] *The Rainbow Road* by Hu Qi,[2] *The Cricket* by Ren Dalin, *Little Pang and Little Song* by Gao Xiangzhen, *Lu Xiaogang and Her Little Sister* by Ren Daxing, *Little Groom and Uncle Big Boots* by Zhu Yiyan, *Little Sister Goes to School* by Zhang Youde, *At the Seaside* by Xiao Ping[3] and *The Story of Little Black Horse* by Yuan Jing.[4] Excellent work appeared again after the fall of the "gang of four", including the short stories "Little Wei" by Qu Hang, "The Children on the Steps" by Ming Lianjun, "The Winding Stream" by Cheng Yuan, "The Violin That Is Out of Tune" by Fang Guorong, "The Story of the Tractor" by Luo Chensheng, "Who Will Be the Future Company Leader?" by Wang Anyi, "Bai Lianlian" by You Fengwei and "What Teacher Ma Likes" by Mei Zihan; the novels *Exploring the Sea of Clouds* by Liu Xianping, *Strange Flower* by Chen Mo, *Altai-Ali* by Zhao Yanyi, *Descendents of the Manshuai Tribes* by Peng Jingfeng, *The Mountain Valley Where Wild Bees Swarm* by Li Di and *At Summer Camp* by Su Jin; and the short novels *The Blue Elephant-Trunk Lake* by Zhang Kunhua and *Flowers Open Towards Her* by Luo Chensheng.

SCIENCE FICTION:

Science fiction is a kind of fantasy literature which developed in China after the founding of the new republic. The pioneer of scientific literature for children in China is Gao Shiqi, whose poems on science are a landmark in the history of contemporary Chinese litera-

---

[1] English translation published by FLP, 1974.

[2] English translation published by FLP, 1981.

[3] English translation in *Chinese Literature*, 1957, 1 and published by FLP, 1957.

[4] English translation published by FLP, 1979.

ture. "Our Earth Mother", "Father Time", and "The Secret of Lilliput" not only introduce scientific knowledge to children but are brilliant intellectual exercises in their own right. Science fiction for children has increased in the last few years along with the development of scientific and technical education; *Xiaoling Travels Through the Future* and *Round and Square* by Ye Yonglie, *Flying to Sagittarius* by Zhang Wenguang and *Magic Flute on Snow Mountain* by Tong Enzheng have all been popular.

PICTURE BOOKS:

Picture books for very young children include excellent works such as *The Little Tadpole Looks for Its Mother* by Fang Huizhen and Sheng Lude, *How the Turnip Came Back* by Fang Yiqun[1] and *How the Foal Crossed the Stream* by Peng Wendi.[2] *A Piece of Rubber* by An Weibang and *Silly Little Brother* by Li Datong are popular among children.

(3) NATIONAL ORGANIZATIONS FOR LITERARY RESEARCH
Societies

Name	Date Founded	President	Address
Society for the Study of Pre-Modern Chinese Literary Theory	December 1979	Guo Shaoyu	Fudan University, Shanghai
Society for Research on Contemporary Chinese Literature	July 1979	Feng Mu	Institute of Literature, Chinese Academy of Social Sciences, Beijing

[1] English translation published by FLP, 1963.
[2] English translation published by FLP, 1976.

Name	Date Founded	President	Address
Society for Research on Chinese Folk Literature	November 1979	Zhou Yang	*Folk Literature*, Beijing
Society for Research on Lu Xun	November 1979	Zhou Yang	Institute of Literature, Chinese Academy of Social Sciences
Society for the Study of Ethnic Minority Literature	June 1979	Zhou Yang (Honorary President) Jia Zhi (President)	As above
National Society for the Study of Foreign Literature	December 1978	Feng Zhi	Institute of Foreign Literature, Chinese Academy of Social Sciences
Society for Research on Comparative Literature	January 1981	Ji Xianlin	Beijing University
Society for Research on Japanese Literature	September 1979	Lin Lin	Institute of Foreign Literature, Chinese Academy of Social Sciences
National Society for Research on American Literature	September 1979	Wu Fuheng	Shandong University, Ji'nan

Name	Date Founded	President	Address
National Society for Research on Literary Theory in Institutes of Higher Learning	1979	Chen Huangmei	East China Normal University, Shanghai
National Society for Research on Soviet Literature	September 1979	Ye Shuifu	Institute of Foreign Literature, Chinese Academy of Social Sciences
National Society for Research on Hispanic Literature	October 1979	Wang Yangle	As above
Northeast Regional Society for Pre-Modern Literature	1981	Yang Gongji	
Society for Research on Taiwan and Hong Kong Literature	February 1981	Zeng Minzhi	Ji'nan University, Guangzhou
Chinese Society for Research on Children's Literature	July 1980	Chen Zijun	Chinese Department, Beijing Normal University
Chinese Society for the Study of *A Dream of Red Mansions*	July 1980	Wu Zuxiang	Institute of *A Dream of Red Mansions*

Name	Date Founded	President	Address
Society for Research on Mao Zedong's Thinking on Literature and Art	1980	Zhang Songru	Chinese Department, Jilin University
Society for the Study of Contemporary Chinese Literature	July 1980	Yao Xueyin	Chinese Department, Zhongshan University
Society for Research on Reportage Literature	August 1980	Xu Chi	Wuhan Normal College
Society for Research on International Reportage Literature	September 1980	Wei Wei	Editorial Board, *Reports on the Times,* Beijing
Society for Research on Su Shi	September 1980	Yang Mingzhao	Chinese Department, Sichuan University

The Institute of Literature and the Institute of Foreign Literature at the Chinese Academy of Social Sciences

The Institute of Literature (founded February 1952)

Director: Sha Ting

Divisions: Literary Theory, Contemporary Literature, Modern Literature, Lu Xun, Early Modern Literature, Folk Literature and the editorial board of *Literary Review*.

The Institute of Foreign Literature (founded 1964)
Director: Feng Zhi
Divisions: Oriental Literature, Western Literature, Soviet Literature, Eastern European Literature and the editorial board of *World Literature*.

The Chinese Academy of the Arts
The Institute of Foreign Literature and Art
Acting Director: Lu Meilin
The Institute of *A Dream of Red Mansions*
Director: Tao Jianji

Literary Research Organizations in Institutes of Higher Learning Fifty-eight organizations for research on literature have been established by 40 comprehensive universities and colleges. Areas covered include the following:

1. Pre-modern Chinese literature: Classical Chinese literature, Yuan, Ming and Qing literature, Tang literature, Tang poetry, Yuan, Ming and Qing fiction and drama, etc.

2. Early modern and modern literature: Modern literature, early modern literature, Lu Xun, Mao Dun, Guo Moruo, Soviet base area literature, etc.

3. Contemporary literature: *Li Zicheng*, contemporary writers from Shanxi, children's literature, reportage literature, etc.

4. Ethnic minority literature: Xinjiang ethnic minority literature, Yunnan ethnic minority literature, Guangxi ethnic minority literature, etc.

5. Literary theory.

There are also organizations for research on foreign

literature, covering Western literature, Russian literature, English and American literature, Oceanic literature, Soviet and Eastern European literature and Southeast Asian literature. The majority of these organizations have been established in the last few years, following the development of the literary and educational professions.

(4) ORGANIZATIONS OF CHINESE WRITERS

The Chinese Federation of Writers and Artists. The Chinese Federation of Writers and Artists is a national federation of writers' and artists' associations. All national-level writers' and artists' associations, research societies and branch federations of writers and artists at provincial, municipal and autonomous regional levels are eligible for membership. The federation is responsible for carrying out coordination, liaison and guidance among its member associations.

The duties of the Federation are:

1. To adopt measures to organize a broad spectrum of writers and artists to come into closer contact with life, to study Marxism, Leninism and Mao Zedong Thought, exchange creative experiences and emulate the good examples set by others, and raise the ideological and artistic standards in literature and the arts;

2. To organize and encourage writers and artists to initiate creative work, theoretical studies and criticism, encourage free competition and debate, and give awards and commendations to excellent creative work, performance, research, teaching and other achievements in literature and the arts;

3. To take positive steps to discover and foster new talent and enlarge the ranks of writers and artists;

4. To respect the traditions and characteristics of the literature and arts of all ethnic groups in China, respect and foster their writers and artists, and promote interchange between their literatures and arts;

5. To strengthen the close relationship between Party and non-Party writers and artists, and strengthen contacts and unity with patriotic writers, artists and their organizations among Chinese compatriots from Taiwan, Hong Kong and Macao and overseas Chinese, forming broadly based alliances with writers and artists who are socialist, patriotic and uphold the national unity of China;

6. To organize and mobilize its member associations to open up international cultural exchanges, form broadly based alliances with writers and artists from other countries, and increase friendly contacts and exchange experiences with them, in order to enrich and improve Chinese literature and the arts, and make a contribution to the development of world culture;

7. To protect the constitutionally guaranteed democratic rights of writers and artists and guarantee freedom for writers and artists to practise creative work, research and international cultural exchanges; when the legitimate rights of writers and artists are illegally encroached upon, it has the responsibility of adopting protective measures and making a direct appeal to the judiciary;

8. To conduct measures to promote the material well-being and interests of writers and artists, to help writers and artists improve their working and living conditions, and assist writers and artists who have special difficulties due to age or illness.

The Chinese Federation of Writers and Artists was founded in July 1949 at the First National Congress of Personnel in Literature and the Arts. The National Committee is in Beijing. At the Fourth Congress in November 1979, Mao Dun (died 1981), was elected honorary president and Zhou Yang was elected president.

At present there are 10 member organizations in the Federation: the Chinese Writers' Association, the Chinese Theatre Artists' Association, the Chinese Film Artists' Association, the Chinese Artists' Association, the Chinese Musicians' Association, the Chinese Dancers' Association, the Chinese Quyi Artists' Association, the Society for Research on Chinese Folk Literature, the Chinese Photographers' Association and the Chinese Variety Artists' Association. There are also branches of the Federation at provincial, municipal and autonomous regional levels.

The Chinese Writers' Association The Chinese Writers' Association is a specialist organization of a mass nature formed voluntarily by Chinese writers. Membership is open to all who endorse the constitution of the Association, to writers who have published literary work, literary theory, criticism or research which reaches a certain standard, and to those who have made distinct achievements in translation, editing, teaching or organization in regard to literary work. Membership is granted upon individual application, introduction by two members or recommendation by a local branch, following ratification from the central presidium.

The Chinese Writers' Association was founded in July 1949 at the First National Congress of Personnel in Literature and the Arts. Its publications include *People's Literature, The Literary Gazette, Poetry, Ethnic Literature* and *The New Observer.* Local branch associations also publish monthly literary journals and there are altogether more than 60 association journals throughout the country.

Mao Dun was President of the Association up to his death in 1981 and Ba Jin its First Vice-President.

(5) LITERARY EXCHANGES WITH FOREIGN COUNTRIES

Since the founding of New China, following the elevation of China's international standing and the development of the literary profession in China, literary exchanges also developed between China and the rest of the world. In the 17 years before the "cultural revolution", the Chinese Writers' Association established close ties with writers and writers' organizations in other countries, carried out regular visits and exchanges, and published translations of a large number of well-known ancient and modern literary works from other countries. During the "cultural revolution", Chinese writers were isolated from the rest of the world for more than 10 years. After 1976, following the restoration of the Chinese Writers' Association, the revival of the literary profession and the development of relations between China and other countries, exchanges between Chinese and foreign writers developed speedily, with great increases in the exchange of visits between Chinese and foreign writers and the translation and presentation of foreign literature. Chinese writers also took part in International P.E.N. Club and other international conferences.

Visits Between Chinese and Foreign Writers Visits between Chinese and foreign writers are an important means of literary exchange. In the last few years, there has been great progress in the number and scope of visits compared with the past. From 1978 through the first half of 1980, the Chinese Writers' Association sent 11 delegations to visit or take part in international conferences in Japan, France, Switzerland, America, Romania, Yugoslavia, West Germany, Australia and Italy, in which more than 60 writers were involved. For example, in April 1979 a delegation headed by Zhou Yang visited Japan, another headed by Ba Jin visited France and another headed by Cao Yu visited Switzerland; their activities had a broad and positive impact in furthering mutual friendship and cooperation. In the same year, a writers' delegation headed by Yan Chen visited Romania; Ye Junjian and Huang Gang were invited to visit Yugoslavia; Xiao Qian and Bi Shuowang were invited to take part in a China Weekend forum at the University of Iowa; and the well-known poet Ai Qing accompanied a delegation of the Chinese Association for Friendship with Foreign Countries on a visit to West Germany, Austria and Italy. In 1980, a delegation of 12 led by Ba Jin paid a 17-day visit to Japan, visiting six cities including Tokyo, Kyoto and Hiroshima; and a delegation led by Yang Xianyi visited Australia to attend the Writers' Week during the Biennial Adelaide Festival of the Arts, meeting writers and artists from Australia, Britain, America, West Germany, Japan, Sweden, India and Malaysia, and discussed projects for the translation and presentation of each other's literary works; a delegation of six writers headed by Liu Baiyu attended a conference on literature of the Yan'an period (1937-1945) in Paris at the invitation of the Foundation Singer-Polignac, giving a presentation to over 30 writers and critics from North America, Europe, Southeast Asia and Hong Kong, on revolutionary literature in the Yan'an base area and progressive literature in the rear areas during the War of Resistance, and afterwards visited Italy at the invitation of the Italian Writers' Association; and a writers' delegation led by Feng Mu visited Bonn, Munich and Cologne at the invitation of the West German writer, Erwin Wickert.

In the last few years, the Chinese Writers' Association has also received a great number of writers and other figures connected with literature and the arts from Canada, Japan, France, the United States and other countries. During 1978 and 1979, 90 meetings and discussions involving more than 300 people were held between Chinese writers and visiting writers and other figures connected with cultural activities. After the Fourth National Congress of Personnel in Literature and the Arts, the Chinese Writers' Association held a meeting for more than 100 foreign writers, critics, translators and other figures and specialists in cultural matters then working in Beijing, to report on the work of the congress and answer questions.

International P.E.N. Club Activities The International P.E.N. Club, founded in 1921, is one of the earliest international writers' organizations. Its headquarters is in London and there are 83 P.E.N. Centres in five continents (including the Eastern European countries but excluding the Soviet Union). On 17 April, 1980 China founded a P.E.N. Centre and sent Chen Huangmei, Zhu Ziqi and Ye Junjian to attend the 1980 annual meeting of the International P.E.N. Club in Yugoslavia. The conference passed a motion admitting China as a member of International P.E.N. On behalf of Chinese writers, Chen Huangmei expressed his respect for the work of International P.E.N. and international cultural exchange, and

China's sincere wish for cooperation with world authors. His speech was welcomed by all participants.

Foreign Literature in China and Translations of Chinese Literature In the last 30 years, China has published translations of a great number of well-known literary works from other countries, among them the plays of the three great Greek tragedians, Goethe's *Faust,* and representative works by famous authors such as Schiller, Shakespeare, Balzac, Tolstoy, Turgenev, Maupassant, Dickens, Mark Twain, Kobayashi Takiji and Gorky, poetry by Heine, Shelly, Whitman, Pushkin, Lermontov, Petöfi, Tagore and Mayakovsky, and fairy tales by the Brothers Grimm and Hans Christian Andersen.

Since 1976, increased attention has been paid to the presentation of works from other countries, especially in contemporary literature. The People's Literature Press and the Shanghai Translation Press have plans to publish a series of Marxist works on literary theory, a series of foreign works on literary theory, a series of famous world classics and so on. The People's Literature Press also has plans to compile 30-volume collections of literature from Japan, India and northern Europe; it will also compile a series on modern drama in 10 volumes; the collected works of Gorky in 20 volumes; the selected works of Dostoievsky in six volumes; and short story collections by several German writers and short story collections by writers from Japan, Australia and Latin America. Work is now in progress on *Les Fleurs du mal* by Baudelaire, poetry by well-known modern French poets, and a selection of Goethe's lyrics. The Foreign Literature Press will publish translations of 40 contemporary literary works from countries all over the world.

Kin Dynasty (1115-1234) model of a theatrical performance excavated in Houma, Shanxi (reproduction).

Yuan Dynasty (1271-1368) wall painting of actors on stage, from Yingtian Monastery in Hongdong, Shanxi.

Scenes from famous Beijing Operas:

The King Bids Farewell to His Concubine.

Reconciliation Between the General and the Minister.

Reed Marsh.

Uproar in Heaven.

A scene from *A Game Yet to Finish,* a colour feature film jointly produced by China and Japan, on the joys and misfortunes experienced by two families of *go* players, one Chinese and one Japanese, against the background of the Anti-Japanese War. The film recounts the sufferings caused by the Japanese war of aggression against China and praises the friendship between the people of the two countries.

A scene from the T.V. mini-series *Marco Polo,* a Chinese-Italian co-production, retracing the steps of Marco Polo, the great 13th-century Venetian traveller. The sequence on Marco Polo in China was filmed at some of China's most scenic spots, including the Great Wall, the Summer Palace, the imperial summer resort in Chengde, the Inner Mongolian grasslands and picturesque Guilin. This still from the film shows Marco Polo disembarking from a dragon boat on his way to an audience with Kublai Khan, emperor of the Yuan Dynasty.

Two stills from the wide-screen animated film *Nezha Stirs Up the Sea*. Chinese animated films enjoy considerable international prestige. Eighteen Chinese animated films have won 26 prizes at international film festivals.

A Northern Wei (386-534) mural depicting a hunt, found in Cave 249 of the Dunhuang Grottoes.

Horses by the famous painter Xu Beihong.

etail from the famous Northern Song (960-1127) painting *Riverside Scene at the Qingming Festival* by Zhang Zeduan. This long horizontal scroll, measuring 525 cm by 25 cm, portrays 770 human figures, 90 animals, 100 buildings, 20 boats, 170 trees and an arched bridge with an unusual structure.

Chicks by the famous painter Qi Baishi.

A Spectacle of Clouds, a view of Huangshan, by the famous painter Liu Haisu.

The six-year-old painter Wang Yani at work.

A painting by Wang Yani at the age of five (1981).

Ivory carvings from the Neolithic Age excavated at Hemudu Village in Yuyao, Zhejiang. The upper left piece has a design of two birds and a sun, carefully executed in flowing lines.

Handicrafts:

Jade carving.

Stone carving.

Lacquer vases.

Porcelain tea set.

Straw and wicker baskets.

Bamboo bird cages.

A stand of bronze bells excavated from a tomb of the Warring States period (475-221 B.C.). Each bell can produce two tones three intervals apart and altogether the bells can produce a range of more than five octaves divided into over 90 musical tones.

Carpets.

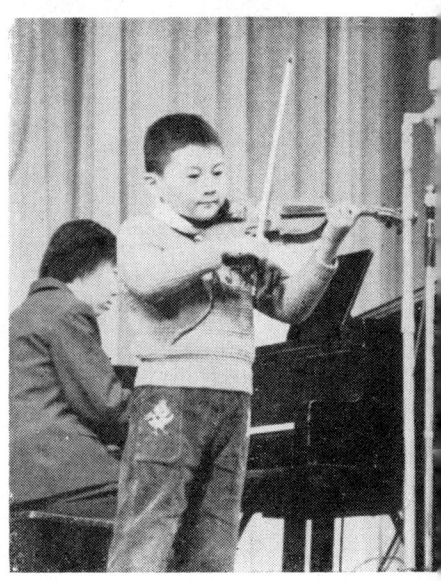

Young musical talents: Wu Man (14) plays the *pipa* lute, Lü Siqing (8), the violin, and Nie Ying (14), the trumpet.

Li Guyi, a popular singer, performing for a rural audience.

Lily Flowers, a Qiang ethn[ic]
dance about Qiang girls joyful[ly]
looking forward to a bright futu[re]

A painted pottery bowl from the Neolithic Age excavated at Shangsunzhai in Datong, Qinghai. It has a design of dancers with linked hands.

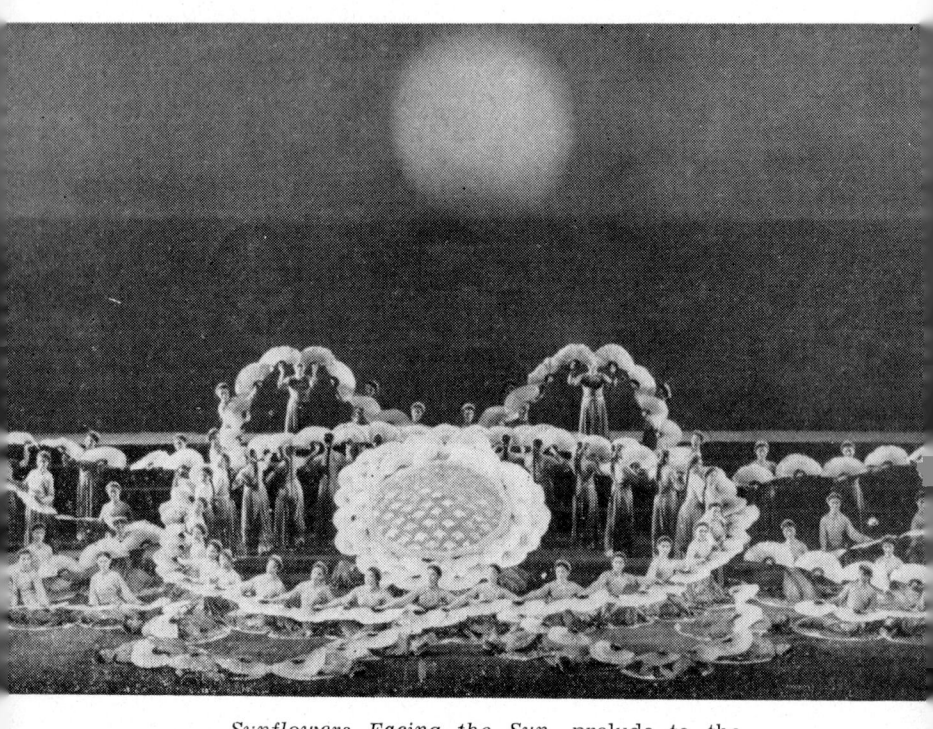

Sunflowers Facing the Sun, prelude to the song and dance epic *The East Is Red*.

Dances by Chen Ailian: *(upper row from left to right)* *Rainbow Skirts and Feathered Robes, Spring Moonlight* and *Flowers on the River and Water;* *(lower row from left to right)* pas de deux from *Princess Wencheng,* the death of the swan from *Swan Lake* and the Spanish dance from *Don Quixote.* Chen Ailian began to make a name for herself in the early sixties when she participated in the dance competition at the Eighth World Youth Festival where she won four gold medals. She has since further developed her skills to new heights.

Gao Yuanjun, a famous Shandong *Kuaishu* (ballad) performer.

Luo Yusheng, a famous *jingyun dagu* (Beijing Drumsong) performer.

Hou Baolin (*left*) and Guo Quanbao, two famous *xiangsheng* performers, doing a comic dialogue.

Acrobatics: Handstands on stacked chairs and trick-cycling (with 14 women on one bicycle).

Chinese acrobats performing abroad.

There are also several journals edited and published in China which translate literary works from other countries, such as *World Literature* and *Works in Translation*. In the past few years, following the increase of Sino-foreign cultural exchange and the further strengthening of research in foreign literature, new journals have been published such as *Research on Foreign Literature,* edited by the Society for Research on Foreign Literature, *Research on Contemporary American Literature,* edited at Shandong University, *Contemporary Foreign Literature*, edited at Nanjing University, *Russian and Soviet Literature,* edited at Wuhan University, *Foreign Literature,* edited at the Beijing Foreign Languages Institute and *Literature Abroad* edited at Beijing University.

Many well-known Chinese works from the past and present have also been translated into many foreign languages for distribution abroad, such as the famous novels *A Dream of Red Mansions, Outlaws of the Marsh* and *The Scholars,* fiction, poetry and drama by modern authors such as Lu Xun, Guo Moruo, Mao Dun, Ba Jin and Lao She, and excellent contemporary works such as *Builders of a New Life* by Liu Qing, *The Song of Youth* by Yang Mo, *Tracks in the Snowy Forest* by Qu Bo and *Red Crag* by Luo Guangbin and Yang Yiyan. The magazine *Chinese Literature,* published in two editions, English and French, presents Chinese literature abroad and is now distributed in 135 countries and regions around the world.

Chapter Two

THE ARTS

1. THEATRE

China has one of the longest and richest histories of theatre in the world, including more than 360 traditional local operas, over 60 kinds of shadow and puppet theatres, and 460 kinds of modern drama (spoken drama), opera, dance-drama and ethnic minority theatrical forms. These distinctive forms of Chinese theatre, with roots that go deep into mass culture, constitute an important component of the cultural life of the Chinese people and occupy a secure place in world theatre.

(1) TRADITIONAL CHINESE OPERA

Beijing Opera and Local Opera The origins of Chinese theatre go far back into Chinese history. Around the 13th century a type of theatre arose that combined acting, singing, dialogue and acrobatics with artistically mature scripts and performance techniques. Known to the rest of the world as "Chinese opera", this tradition formed the mainstream of Chinese theatre up to modern times. Over the years many different varieties of Chinese opera emerged as well as many regional variations. Recent surveys have found 368 different forms of opera throughout the country, and every province and autonomous region has one or more forms of local opera. Among the best-known forms staged nationwide are Beijing Opera, Pingju (found mainly in north China), Shaoxing Opera (mainly in Zhejiang and Shanghai) and Yuju (Henan Clapper Opera, mainly in Henan Province). Strictly speaking all forms of traditional opera, including Beijing Opera, are "regional" in that they are based on the music and dialects of specific areas and therefore their popularity is largely confined to that area. In contemporary Chinese studies, however, Beijing Opera is usually regarded as a national form, and all others are classified as "local opera".

Beijing Opera commands the largest following in China and is also the best-known form of Chinese opera abroad. It assumed its present form in the mid-19th century in Beijing, then capital of the Qing Dynasty. The music of Beijing Opera is based on the *erhuang* tune family from Huiju (Anhui Opera) and the *xipi* tune family from Hanju (Hubei Opera). It also incorporates some of the repertoire, tunes and musical accompaniment of Kunqu (Kunshan Opera), Qinqiang (Shaanxi Clapper Opera) and folk music. In short, the best of all existing performing arts have been combined to form an artistically advanced form of theatre, in which equal attention is given to singing, dialogue, acting and acrobatics. Traditional Chinese string and percussion instruments provide a strongly rhythmical accompaniment. The acting in Beijing Opera is based on illusion: gestures, footwork and other body movements express actions such as riding a horse, rowing a boat, opening a door, going up stairs, climbing a hill and travelling, and are themselves aesthetically satisfying. Spoken dialogue is divided into two kinds, *yunbai* (recitative speech) and *jingbai* (Beijing colloquial speech), the former employed by serious characters and the latter by young females and clowns; both are declaimed with much emphasis, rhythm, clarity and force.

The character roles in Beijing Opera are finely and strictly differentiated into fixed types. Female roles are generally known as *dan* and male roles as *sheng,* but male clowns are known as *chou,* and vigorous male roles as *jing* or *hua lian* (painted faces). Female roles can be subdivided into *qingyi* (refined young or middle-aged women), *huadan* (flirtatious girls or young women), *wudan* or *daomadan* (women with martial skills), *laodan* (old women), and *caidan* (female clowns). Male roles can also be subdivided into different types. Each of these role types has its own singing and acting style.

The traditional repertoire of Beijing Opera includes more than 1,000 items, mostly taken from traditional historical novels about political and military struggles, such as *Outlaws of the Marsh, Romance of the Three Kingdoms* and *Generals of the Yang Family.* Among the most popular items are *The Empty City Ruse, The Gathering of Heroes, Women Generals of the Yang Family, The King Bids Farewell to His Concubine, A Woman Feigning Madness, The Fisherman's Revenge, At the Crossroads* and *Uproar in Heaven.*

In the course of the development of Beijing Opera, a number of talented actors created highly distinctive singing and acting techniques, adapting the traditional skills learned from their masters to take advantage of their own abilities and giving rise to different schools. The very influential Mei School, for instance, was founded by the most famous Beijing Opera actor of modern times, Mei Lanfang, who made continuous improvements to singing, movement, recitative, music, costumes and make-up in the course of many years of stage performance. His repertoire included *A Woman Feigning Madness*, *The Drunken Beauty* and *The King Bids Farewell to His Concubine*. Among other well-known Beijing Opera actors are Cheng Yanqiu, Zhou Xinfang, Ma Lianliang, Tan Fuying, Gai Jiaotian and Zhang Junqiu.

In the 30-odd years since the founding of the People's Republic, tremendous achievements have been made in reforming Beijing Opera, sorting out and re-editing traditional items, creating new items on both historical and modern subjects, and making reforms in stagecraft. Beijing Opera is now able to portray contemporary as well as traditional life, thus gaining a new vitality. A new generation of young performers are making new advances on the basis of the traditional schools.

Pingju dates from the end of the Qing and the beginning of the republican era. It originates in a form of folk opera from Hebei, known as Lianhualuo, and later absorbed singing and acting techniques from Hebei Bangzi (clapper opera), Beijing Opera, Luanzhou shadow plays, and Leting Dagu (a verse narrative sung to the accompaniment of a small drum and other instruments). Pingju is popular in Beijing, Tianjin, Hebei and the northeast. Its tunes, dialogue and acting are deeply rooted in people's life, so that it is lively and easy to understand. Since Liberation, Pingju has concentrated on contemporary themes, and it has now become a nationally popular form.

Yuju (Henan Opera) is also known as Henan Bangzi. It originated in local folk plays during the Qing Dynasty, with elements from Shaanxi Opera and Puzhou Bangzi. Around the end of the Qing, Henan Opera spread to cities and under the influence of Beijing Opera became a fully-developed genre popular in Henan, Shaanxi, Shanxi, Hebei, Shandong and Anhui. Its long history in the countryside has given it a lively, simple rural character. Its range of tunes and repertoire are both very rich.

Yueju (Shaoxing Opera) first took shape at the end of the Qing on the basis of folk songs from Shengxian in Zhejiang, incorporating singing and acting techniques of local operas such as Tanhuang and Shaoju. It was later influenced by modern drama and Kunqu and became very popular in Shanghai, Jiangsu and Zhejiang. The soft and gentle music of Shaoxing Opera is most appropriate for sentimental emotions, and the acting style is similarly graceful and refined. After Liberation, the former all-female casts were replaced by mixed casts and the vocal music was reformed accordingly. It has now gained national popularity.

Qinqiang (Shaanxi Opera), one of the oldest kinds of operas in China, appeared during the Ming Dynasty. The singing is loud and clear, and the clapper accompaniment has a strong rhythm. The acting is also plain and vigorous. It was widely popular around the end of the Ming and the beginning of the Qing, influencing to different degrees many other types of local opera. Its introduction to Henan, Shanxi, Hebei and Shandong produced a series of clapper operas based on local dialects and folk songs. Shaanxi Opera now enjoys big audiences in Shaanxi, Gansu and Qinghai, and its traditional repertoire includes over 2,000 items.

Kunqu (Kunshan Opera) is one of the oldest operatic forms in China. It originated in the Kunshan area of Jiangsu around the end of the Yuan Dynasty and the early Ming, and received its definitive form in late Ming.

Kunqu singing is gentle and clear, its tunes are beautiful and refined, and its stage movements resemble dancing. It reached its peak of popularity at the end of the Ming and the early period of the Qing, exerting tremendous impact on other types of opera. Around the middle of the Ming Dynasty it spread to the north and gradually developed into a more vigorous and rugged type of opera known as Northern Kunqu. Towards the end of the Qing, however, Kunqu declined because it had become too refined and elegant. After Liberation, Kunqu gained a new life, with reforms in singing style and librettos making it more straightforward and suited to popular taste.

Chuanju (Sichuan Opera) is the major form of local opera in southwestern China, popular in Sichuan, Guizhou and Yunnan. It appeared around the middle of the Qing Dynasty out of a combination of several local opera forms such as Kunqu, Gaoqiang, Huqin, Tanxi and Dengxi. Its most characteristic feature is its high-pitched singing style. The repertoire is very rich, totalling over 2,000 items. The scripts are of high literary value and are noted for their humour. The acting style is meticulous and very expressive.

Hanju (Hubei Opera) is an old operatic form originating in Hubei. It dates back more than 300 years and has had much influence on the formation of Beijing Opera, Sichuan Opera and Xiangju (Hunan Opera). Its vocal music, mainly from the *xipi* and *erhuang* tune families, has many musical patterns and over 400 tune names. The repertoire is also very large. Hanju is popular in Hubei, Henan, Shaanxi and Hunan.

Yueju (Guangzhou Opera) first appeared in the Qing Dynasty, originally under the influence of Kunqu and

Yiyangqiang (another old opera type) and later absorbing elements from Anhui Opera, Hubei Opera and Guangdong folk tunes. Thanks to the rich assortment of musical instruments employed, its varied tunes and its readiness to innovate, the opera has grown rapidly to become a major operatic form in Guangdong and Guangxi and also among overseas Chinese communities in Southeast Asia and America.

Chaoju (Chaozhou Opera) is an old operatic form that dates back to the middle of the Ming Dynasty. It still retains some elements of the Song and Yuan Nanxi (Southern Drama, originating in Jiangsu and Zhejiang) and older music. The singing style is rich and beautiful. Characteristic features are the acrobatic clowning, using fans and leg movements, and all kinds of lifelike mimicry. Chaoju draws big audiences in the Chaozhou-Shantou region in Guangdong, southern parts of Fujian and overseas Chinese communities in Southeast Asia.

Liyuanxi (Pear Garden Drama) is an old operatic form closely related to Song and Yuan Nanxi. It originated in the Quanzhou and Xiamen areas of Fujian and is popular where the southern Fujian dialect is spoken, including Taiwan and overseas Chinese communities in Southeast Asia. Liyuanxi is divided into major and minor types, the former drawing mainly on Nanxi drama and the latter on folk tales. The singing is beautiful and the acting has characteristic stage walks and body movements. After Liberation, the two types of Liyuanxi were merged to enrich the repertoire and singing style.

Tibetan Opera, based on Tibetan folk songs and dances, first appeared towards the end of the 14th century, and developed into an influential ethnic opera in the 17th century. It is popular with Tibetan communities in Tibet, Sichuan, Qinghai and southern Gansu. The librettos mostly consist of folk ballads and the tunes are fixed. The singing is high-pitched and loud and is accompanied by a chorus. Some characters wear masks. Tibetan Opera is usually performed in open-air squares. Its traditional repertoire includes full-length items based on folk and Buddhist stories, such as *Princess Wen Cheng* and *Prince Norsang*, as well as small skits with singing and dancing.

Puppet theatre goes back more than 2,000 years. The many varieties include marionettes, rod puppets, cloth puppets and wire puppets. The performance incorporates folk songs and dances. The movements are based on dance steps and the singing mostly on local opera tunes. Some forms also have dialogue. The subject-matter used to be taken from historical stories and myths but are now mostly from children's stories, fables and modern life. The performers usually work as a team, one with the task of manipulating the puppets, another singing and reciting, and a third playing the music, but there are also performers who can put on a one-man show. The Chinese puppet theatre has an international reputation.

Shadow plays (also known as lantern silhouette shows) are performed by moving figures made of animal skins or cardboard held behind a screen lit by lamplight. They are closely related to local operas in regard to subject-matter and singing style. The performers simultaneously sing, accompany themselves instrumentally and manipulate the puppets. There are many types of shadow plays, depending on the area where it is popular, the kind of music and singing, and the different materials used to make the figures. Among the best-known are the donkey-skin shadow plays of Luanxian in Hebei, and the ox-skin shadow plays in the northwest. After Liberation, some outstanding shadow plays were made into animated films which were well received both at home and abroad.

Development of Traditional Opera in New China Soon after the founding of New China in 1949, one of the primary tasks of the Ministry of Culture was to introduce democratic reforms in opera troupes, improve the livelihood of opera personnel and raise their social status. At the same time, a bureau was set up to guide reforms in opera. A government directive on opera reform was issued in 1951, stating that the foremost task of opera is to develop the people's patriotism and encourage the heroism displayed by the people in revolutionary struggles and productive labour. The encouragement of slave ethics, barbarity, violence or indecency was to be opposed, as also derogatory portrayals of working people. The directive set forth the policy of encourging free competition among different operatic forms and fostering local operas. A national opera festival was held in 1952, at which more than 1,000 people representing 23 operatic forms presented nearly 100 traditional plays and discussed their experiences in opera reform. Regional festivals were subsequently staged in the provinces and municipalities to promote opera reform.

Great successes were made in investigating, rearranging and analysing the traditional repertoire of various forms of opera. By 1957, the operatic repertoire was greatly enriched. A total of 51,867 traditional items had been noted, 1,400 scripts recorded, and 4,200 scripts rearranged. Thanks to much diligent work, well over 100 fine plays had been staged, including *The White Snake* (Beijing Opera), *Liang Shanbo and Zhu Yingtai* (Shaoxing Opera), *Love Under the Willows* (Sichuan Opera) and *The Orphan of the Zhao Family* (Shaanxi Opera). Assessments of performing skills were gradually being carried out, and accounts by leading performers of their experiences were published, such as Mei Lanfang's *Forty Years of Stage Life*, Cheng Yanqiu's *Writings by Cheng Yanqiu* and Gai Jiaotian's *Grease-paint Chronicles*.

In the wake of the investigation into traditional operas, many forms that had been on the brink of extinction before Liberation were revived, such as Kunqu, Hebei Bangzi, Anhui Opera and Yiyang Opera. With the help of the Ministry of Culture and its branches, some ethnic minorities which previously had no theatre of their own now created new kinds of opera based on local folk music and drawing on other local operas. Zhuang Opera (from Guangxi), Dai Opera (from Yunnan) and Miao Opera (from Hunan) are all new kinds of local opera. In addition, new operatic forms appeared throughout the country, such as Quju Opera (based on Dagu), Jilin Opera (based on Errenzhuan, a traditional local opera from the northeast) and Tangshan Opera (based on Tangshan shadow plays).

Outstanding achievements were made in writing and staging new operas on historical and modern themes, opening up a broad road for the development of traditional Chinese opera. In the first years after Liberation, troupes throughout the country wrote new operas on historical themes and began to investigate writing operas on modern themes, while continuing to perform their traditional repertoire. The first results of these investigations were seen in local opera, such as *Arhat Coins* (Huju, or Shanghai Opera), *Liu Qiao'er* (Pingju), *The Re-*

marriage of Sister Li Er (Lüju Opera), *A Chicken Feather Flies to the Sky* (Shaoxing Opera) and *Chaoyanggou* (Henan Opera), all good operas on modern themes. In 1960, the policy of equal stress on modern operas, traditional operas and new historical operas was announced, followed by discussions among opera personnel on historical operas and Beijing operas on modern themes. The creation of new historical operas and operas on modern themes advanced to a new stage. Ideologically and artistically mature new operas on historical themes, for instance, included the Beijing operas *Xie Yaohuan* and *Hai Rui's Dismissal from Office*. Local operas on modern themes also improved, resulting in outstanding works such as *Sparks Amid the Reeds* (Shanghai Opera), *The Bronze Gong* and *The Tinker* (Flower-Drum Opera), and *A Visit Home* (Quju), all from the 1960s. A breakthrough was also made in efforts to create Beijing operas on modern themes. In the nationwide Beijing Opera festival in 1964, 28 Beijing Opera troupes presented 37 operas on modern themes. *The Red Lantern, Sparks Amid the Reeds, Jie Zhenguo, No. 6 Gate, Azalea Mountain, Raid on the White Tiger Regiment* and *Daino* all drew favourable comment from the audience.

The training of new opera personnel also received much attention. Opera schools were set up throughout the country and many local opera troupes also ran classes to train their own young talents. By the time of the "cultural revolution", two-thirds of the 200,000 opera personnel had received their training since 1949.

However, in the winter of 1965, Jiang Qing, Kang Sheng and their allies mounted a long-deliberated campaign against *Hai Rui's Dismissal from Office*. This was in fact the prelude to the "cultural revolution". During the "cultural revolution", opera was a chief target of attack and suffered grave damage. Most local opera troupes were disbanded, performers forced to do other work, noted scriptwriters persecuted, and practically all operas banned. For 10 years the stage was dominated by a handful of "model operas".

After the downfall of Jiang Qing's counter-revolutionary clique, local operas and troupes were quickly revived, and the wrongly criticized plays, scriptwriters, directors and performers rehabilitated. "Letting a hundred flowers blossom and weeding through the old to bring forth the new" and other correct policies were once again implemented, and the creation, compilation, re-editing and performance of operas sprang to life again. New progress was made in portraying modern life through opera, and many operas created successful portrayals of old revolutionaries. Some operas won popular acclaim for their high ideological and artistic level in depicting modern life, such as *The Xi'an Incident* (Shaanxi Opera), *Mainstay in the South* and *A Bag of Honey* (Beijing Opera), *Niu Duoxi in a Sedan Chair* (Hunan Flower-Drum Opera) and *The Fourth-Born Sister* (Sichuan Opera). Traditional operas were re-edited and staged again, including the excellent *Women Generals of the Yang Family* and *The White Snake* (Beijing Opera), *Third Sister Liu* (Caidiao), *The Remarriage of Two Sisters* (Shanxi Opera), *Chuncao Storms the Magistrate's Hall* (Puxian Opera), *Judge Bao's Apology* (Jilin Opera), *Rouge* (Shaoxing Opera), and *A Wise Magistrate* (Henan Opera). New operas on historical themes included *Sima Qian the Historian* (Beijing Opera), *Cai Wenji* (Kunqu), *Sleeping Tiger Mountain* (Sichuan Opera), *Lady Shexiang* (Guizhou Opera) and *Yu Qian* (Shaoju). *Hai Rui's Dismissal from*

Office and other plays wrongly criticized during the "cultural revolution" were also restaged.

The number of opera personnel has greatly increased since 1949, despite the damages suffered in the 10 years of domestic turmoil. At present, their number already exceeds 200,000, and there are 3,000 opera troupes as against 1,000 shortly after Liberation. There are also many amateur opera troupes.

(2) SPOKEN DRAMA

The Development of Spoken Drama Plays consisting of dialogue in the vernacular without singing did not exist in the traditional Chinese theatre but were introduced around the time of the 1911 Revolution. To distinguish them from traditional opera they are known as *huaju* (spoken plays) in Chinese. For convenience "spoken plays" will be referred to here collectively as drama. The earliest drama troupe was the Spring Willow Society, founded by Chinese students in Tokyo in 1906. It was followed by the Progressive Troupe, founded in 1910, and the South China Society, founded in 1925, which played an important role in promoting and improving the new drama. The first major successes of the new drama were Cao Yu's *Thunderstorm* and *Sunrise* which had a tremendous impact on society on their performance during the thirties. The War of Resistance Against Japan saw the rise of "street theatre", short plays in colloquial language performed on the streets, which encouraged the people to resist the invaders and save the country. The best-known of these was *Put Down Your Whip*. Many historical plays were also written during the war, the most famous being Guo Moruo's *Qu Yuan* and *Twin Flowers*, which praised patriotism and self-sacrifice and satirized reality, arousing strong sympathy among the people in the Kuomintang-controlled areas. Other important playwrights in the 1930s and 1940s include Tian Han, Ouyang Yuqian, Hong Shen and Xia Yan.

New Achievements of Drama in New China Drama developed fairly rapidly in the first 17 years of the People's Republic, especially in regard to number. A large number of plays appeared on new themes such as the new socialist era and the people's new life. *Never Forget Class Struggle, Facing New Things, The Rising Sun, Happiness* and *Fighting Upstream* depicted the life and struggle of workers; *The Spring Breeze Comes to the Nuomin River, Locust Tree Village, After a Bumper Harvest* and *Green Pine Ridge* were on life in rural areas; *Bright Horizon, The Song of Youth* and *Three Intellectuals* were about ideological remoulding among intellectuals; *Dragon Beard Ditch* and *Saleswomen* were about changes in urban life; *Steeled Transport Troops, Heroic Positions, Sentinels Under Neon Lights, The Second Spring* and *Lei Feng* portrayed the struggles of the Chinese Volunteers and Liberation Army in defence of their homeland; *Song of Bayinaola, At the Foot of the Tianshan Mountains, The Wedding of the Hezhen People* and *On the Kangpur Grassland* were about the struggle and life of the ethnic minorities; and *Look West to Chang'an, Blow the Vertical Flute Traversely* and *Before the Arrival of the New Director* criticized bureaucracy and ideological shortcomings among the people. There were also many historical plays, such as *Cai Wenji, Wu Zetian, Guan Hanqing, Princess Wen Cheng* and *Gou Jian Rebuilds the State* on pre-modern history,

Teahouse, Yihequan and *The Naval Battle of 1894* on social life and the people's struggle in modern times, and numerous plays on the New Democratic Revolution led by the Chinese Communist Party such as *Red Storm, Keep the Red Flag Flying, Across Rivers and Mountains, Flames in July, The Battle of Leopard Valley, The Last Act, Under Siege* and *Prelude to the Eastward March*. Much attention was given to children's plays after 1949. A children's theatre was established and many plays were written and staged, such as *A Revolutionary Family, The Little Footballers, Yue Yun, The Magic Aster* and *The Magic Boat*. Famous works by Guo Moruo, Cao Yu, Tian Han, Xia Yan and other playwrights of the May 4th Movement and after were staged, and also outstanding plays by the famous foreign playwrights Shakespeare, Molière, Schiller, Gogol, Chekhov, Gorki, Ostrovsky, Goldoni and Kalidasa. Drama in China flourished as never before.

Standards in acting, directing and stagecraft were also raised considerably. Dramatists went on study tours abroad, students went abroad for further training and all types of training classes and lectures were arranged. Research was carried out on Stanislavski's and Brecht's theories on drama and acting, and the aesthetics and performing techniques of traditional Chinese opera were also given close attention. A native dramatic style gradually took shape in the early sixties. A number of fine directors and performing artists appeared, together with several drama troupes with strong casts and distinctive styles, such as the Beijing People's Art Theatre, the Chinese Youth Art Theatre, the Central Experimental Drama Theatre, the Chinese Children's Art Theatre, the Shanghai People's Art Theatre, the Liaoning People's Art

Theatre, and two drama troupes in the People's Liberation Army, Comrades and the Frontline. A large number of new actors and actresses were trained in different ways, and in 1966, the number of professional drama personnel exceeded 20,000 and that of professional drama troupes exceeded 160.

During the "cultural revolution", modern drama was condemned by Jiang Qing as "dead drama", all plays branded as "poisonous weeds", and many drama troupes disbanded. In this way the development of modern drama was halted for a whole decade.

After 1976, drama enjoyed a second liberation, entering a new period of development. Over 200 full-length plays were written and staged in the three years 1977-79. About 150 were about the crimes of the Lin Biao and Jiang Qing counter-revolutionary cliques, such as *Loyal Hearts*, *Where There Is Silence*, *When the Maple Leaves Turn Red*, *The City Party Secretary*, *Children's Hearts*, *Rugged Years* and *Storm over China*. Whether comedy, tragedy, satire or children's plays, they exposed from different angles Lin Biao's and Jiang Qing's conspiratorial activities and showed the people's resistance to them. These important plays were welcomed enthusiastically by the masses. A number of other plays from the same period portrayed the feats of proletarian leaders and revolutionary veterans, such as *The Newspaper Boys*, *Turning Point*, *Vicissitudes*, *Dawn*, *March East, March East!* and *The Xi'an Incident*. These plays made artistic breakthroughs in portraying the rich inner minds, noble spiritual worlds and unique characters of China's revolutionary leaders. In the last two years, plays on new problems, new people and new ideas, such as *The Call of the Future*, *Primrose*, *March On, March On!* and *Rights and Law* which show from several aspects the spiritual damage caused by the Lin Biao and Jiang Qing counter-revolutionary cliques and the contradictions among the people in the new period, have had considerable social impact. There have also been plays on international themes, such as *The Other Side*, *The Legend of Chinatown* and *Blood-stained Cherry Blossoms*; revolutionary historical plays such as *Ji Hongchang* and *Growing Up by the Yanhe River*; historical plays such as *Wang Zhaojun* and *Hurricane Song*; and a translated version of *Galileo* by Bertolt Brecht. Plays from the thirties have also been restaged.

A national conference was held on scriptwriting in early 1980 to discuss how to reflect accurately the social contradictions in the new period, the writers' sense of responsibility and the social impact of drama. The conference was very successful in promoting the sound development of scriptwriting. The recent plays *Blood Is Always Warm*, *Neighbours*, *Mayor Chen Yi*, *Late Blossoms* and *Dawn Comes to the Grey Kingdom* not only show a marked improvement in depth of content, the exploration of new subject matter and portrayal of typical characters, but also are inventive and original in regard to artistic presentation and stage performance.

(3) EDUCATION AND RESEARCH IN THE THEATRICAL ARTS

Modern Drama. The two tertiary-level drama schools in China are the Central Drama Institute in Beijing and the Shanghai Drama Institute. They each have four departments (acting, directing, stage design and dramatic literature) and seven concentrations (acting, directing, stage design, lighting, make-up, theory and scriptwriting). The courses last for four years except in the directing concentration where it is five years. They also run training classes in response to national demand. Most of the art institutes and schools in the provinces, municipalities and autonomous regions have drama classes or concentrations for training local drama personnel. Many drama troupes also sponsor courses for training their own young actors and actresses.

Traditional Opera. The Chinese Opera Institute is China's only tertiary-level opera school. It has three departments, Beijing Opera acting, opera directing and opera music. At present, preparations are under way to add departments of Beijing Opera scriptwriting and direction, opera stage design and opera education. The courses last from three to four years. There are also 28 secondary-level opera schools, which enroll 11- and 12-year-olds for a period of seven years. Most of the opera troupes throughout the country run classes for training their own new recruits. The traditional way of training young actors was through the master-apprentice system. This is still adopted as a complementary form of training, and has played a significant role in studying and carrying on the techniques of different schools.

Amateur education is also an important way of training new recruits. Local arts and cultural centres and factories, mines and communes also run amateur opera and drama schools and classes. The most popular method is for the trainees to join amateur troupes where they can study and perform at the same time.

Research on opera and drama is carried out at the opera and drama research institutes of the Chinese Academy of Art.

Several theatrical societies and associations have been established in the last few years, such as the Chinese Puppet and Shadow-Play Arts Society, the Chinese Stage Design Society, the Chinese Society for Research on Radio Drama, and the Chinese Society for Research on Traditional Opera on Modern Themes. Research on the arts of different schools of Beijing Opera is also being conducted, and research groups on the Cheng Yanqiu and Ma Lianliang schools have been set up in Beijing.

(4) THE CHINESE THEATRE ARTISTS' ASSOCIATION

This is a mass voluntary professional organization of Chinese theatrical personnel. Originally called the National Association of Chinese Theatre Personnel, it was established at the First National Congress of Literary and Art Personnel in 1949. It was renamed into the Chinese Theatre Artists' Association in 1953 at the Second National Congress of Literary and Art Personnel. It is open to all Chinese engaged in traditional opera, modern drama, modern opera, children's theatre, shadow plays, puppetry, radio and television drama and ethnic minority opera who support the association's regulations and have achieved high levels in writing, theoretical research, education, editing, organization and popularization in the fields of scriptwriting, directing, acting, opera music and stage design. It publishes the journals *People's Drama, Scripts, Theatre News, Short Scripts* and *Foreign Drama*. Branches of the Association in Shanghai, Liaoning, Heilongjiang, Sichuan, Hebei, Henan, Shaanxi and Anhui also publish journals.

The president of the Association is Cao Yu.

(5) EXCHANGES WITH OTHER COUNTRIES

Since 1949, China has sent many theatrical troupes to international theatrical festivals and youth festivals, winning many awards. Beijing Opera, Shaoxing Opera, Sichuan Opera, Pingju, puppet show and shadow-play troupes from China have performed in over 50 countries and regions, bringing traditional Chinese opera to the people of other lands. Before the "cultural revolution", the Beijing Opera Troupe of China alone performed in more than 40 countries. Dramatists and students have gone abroad for research and study on foreign theatre, foreign experts have been invited to give lectures in China and meetings in commemoration of world-famous playwrights have been held. Cultural exchanges with other countries in the theatrical arts were suspended during the "cultural revolution" and were not resumed until after 1976. In recent years, there has been a steady increase in exchanges of groups and individuals connected with the theatre. In the last three years, the Chinese Theatre Artists' Association has played host to over 30 groups of American, British, French, Japanese, Romanian, Greek, Swedish and Philippine theatre personnel, the National Theatre of Greece, the Old Vic Theatre Company of Britain, the Bungakuza and Seinenza of Japan and the Yugoslav Puppet Troupe. Chinese theatrical troupes such as the Beijing Opera Troupe of Beijing, the Beijing Opera Troupe of Yunnan and the Shaoxing Opera Troupe of Shanghai went on performance tours of the United States, Austria and other countries and regions; and the Beijing People's Art Theatre performed *Teahouse,* the famous modern play by Lao She, in West Germany, Switzerland and France to general acclaim. In the last two years, there have also been several instances of Sino-foreign joint productions in China. In 1981, a British team participated in the Beijing People's Art Theatre production of Shakespeare's *Measure for Measure* with much success. China also sent theatrical delegations to West Germany, Japan, Britain and the United States to study drama and publicize the development of the Chinese theatre.

In 1979 and 1981, Chinese theatrical delegations took part in the Fourth International Theatre Forum in Yugoslavia and the International Brecht Symposium in Hong Kong. The Chinese Centre of the International Drama Union was set up in 1980 as a member of the IDU, an international non-governmental drama organization founded in 1947. The IDU, which has its headquarters in Paris, has 54 member states and holds a convention every two years. In 1981, Zhao Xun and three others from The IDU Chinese Contre participated in the 19th Convention of the IDU in Madrid, where they spoke on the history of Chinese theatre up to the present time and the nature of traditional theatre in China.

2. THE CINEMA

(1) THE EARLY PERIOD (1896-1949)

The cinema was introduced into China in 1896, but it was not until the eve of the First World War that China made its first film. In 1931, a number of fairly progressive films were produced under the leadership or influence of the Chinese Communist Party by writers and artists in Shanghai and other places, including *Plunder of Peach and Plum*, *The Great Road*, *Song of the Fishermen* and *Crossroads*. Film personnel in Kuomintang-controlled areas in the 1930s and 1940s produced another group of films which had a considerable social impact, such as *Along the Songhua River*, *The Spring River Flows East* and *Eight Thousand Li of Cloud and Moon*.

In the liberated areas under the leadership of the Chinese Communist Party, the Yan'an Film Group, founded in September 1938, shot valuable documentaries of the War of Resistance Against Japan and the War of Liberation, such as *Yan'an and the Eighth Route Army*, *Dr. Norman Bethune* and *Nanniwan*. The Northeast Film Studio was established in the Northeast Liberated Area in the autumn of 1946, the first people's studio with fairly complete equipment.

(2) THE DEVELOPMENT OF THE CINEMA IN NEW CHINA

Film Production The film industry made great advances after the founding of New China. In the 17 years between 1949 and 1966, China produced 603 feature films, including filmed stage productions. The excellent films of the 1950s, such as *The White-Haired Girl*, *Steeled Fighters, Reconnaissance Across the Changjiang, Dong Cunrui* and *The Shepherd's Message*, attracted millions of people with their new ideas, new characters and new social values. In particular, the exhibition of new films in October 1959, in celebration of the 10th anniversary of the founding of the People's Republic, showed several films which were diverse in theme and style and of a high ideological and artistic quality, such as *The Song of*

Youth, *Lin Zexu* and *The Storm*, marking a new level in China's feature film production. Further advances in film production were made in the early 1960s, following a decree from the Ministry of Culture in 1961 on the laws of artistic creativity and the promulgation of regulations governing cultural affairs generally and the cinema. Several films of this period were ideologically fairly advanced and of world standards artistically. They include *Keep the Red Flag Flying*, *Li Shuangshuang*, *A Revolutionary Family*, *The Naval Battle of 1894*, *Little Soldier Zhang Ga*, *Serfs*, *The New Year Sacrifice*, *Sisters on Stage*, *Threshold of Spring* and *The Lin Family's Shop*.

Progress was also made in other types of film. A total of 8,342 reels of documentaries and newsreels were shot in the first 17 years after Liberation, recording the achievements of the Chinese people in all fields of endeavour in socialist revolution and construction, and also about life in other countries. Scientific and educational films, which brought to life knowledge about science and technology, reached a total of 1,980 reels in these years.

Animated films received special attention, and altogether 276 reels were made in this period. Chinese animated films are unique in two ways: firstly, they are healthy in content and secondly they are made in a variety of distinctively Chinese styles, drawing chiefly on traditional Chinese paintings, murals, New Year pictures, folk arts and local opera. Some, for instance, have succeeded in reproducing traditional Chinese ink-wash painting onto the screen, and *The Tadpole Looks for His Mother* and *The Cowherd's Flute* enabled the masterpieces of noted artists Qi Baishi and Li Keran to come to life on the screen. This was a pioneering undertaking in film animation and aroused much interest in the film world in China and abroad. Chinese animated films enjoy a high reputation internationally. Eighteen Chinese animated films have won 26 prizes at international film festivals. The puppet *The Magic Paintbrush,* the papercut *Ginseng Girl,* the ink-wash *The Tadpole Looks for His Mother* and the cartoon *Uproar in Heaven* have each won several awards in international film festivals.

In the decade 1966-1976, Lin Biao's and Jiang Qing's counter-revolutionary cliques labelled the overwhelming majority of the films made before the "cultural revolution" as "poisonous weeds", sealing them up and banning their showing. They also persecuted film personnel and deprived many of their right to make films. As a result, only 69 feature films, 36 animated films, 1,473 reels of documentaries and 731 reels of scientific and educational films were made in that decade. Worthy of note is that Chinese newsreel film crews braved enormous risks in January 1976 to shoot scenes of the nation in mourning over the death of Premier Zhou Enlai and preserved these valuable historical records.

Film production entered a new and flourishing stage after 1976. In four years, nearly 250 feature films were produced, covering a wide range of themes. Some of them depicted revolutionary struggles and paid tribute to the older generation of proletarian revolutionaries; some laid bare the damage caused to the country and the people by Lin Biao's and Jiang Qing's counter-revolutionary cliques; others reflected the new mental outlook of the Chinese people striving to modernize their country and paid tribute to the creativeness and high morale of the advanced elements. These films were varied in style of presentation, drawing both on traditional techniques in traditional Chinese fiction, opera and painting and on foreign films, and making active efforts to give Chinese films a truly native character. Successful films made in this period were *Tear Stains, Ji Hongchang, Anxious to Rejoin His Unit, Legend of Tianyun Mountain, Night Rain on Bashan* and *In and Out of Court*.

Some new animated, scientific and educational films, newsreels and documentaries were also quite popular. *Yellow Weasel, The Hairy Boy* and *Buried Hill Oilfield* won awards at international scientific film festivals and *The Perlas* won a prize at an agricultural contest. The ink-wash cartoon *The Cowherd's Flute* carried away the gold medal at the Third International Fairy Tales Film Festival. The full-length documentary *Eternal Glory to Our Beloved Premier Zhou Enlai,* shot by the Central Documentary and Newsreels Film Studio, won the best award for documentaries at the Third "Hundred Flowers" Film Competition in China.

Film Studios There are now 13 feature film studios in China:

Changchun Film Studio, founded 1946;
Beijing Film Studio, founded 1949;
Shanghai Film Studio, founded 1949;
August First Film Studio in Beijing, founded 1952;
Zhujiang Film Studio in Guangzhou, founded 1958;
Xi'an Film Studio, founded 1958;
Emei Film Studio in Chengdu, founded 1958;
Tianshan Film Studio in Urumqi, founded 1958;
Inner Mongolia Film Studio in Hohhot, founded 1958;
Xiaoxiang Film Studio in Changsha, founded 1977;
Guangxi Film Studio in Nanning, founded 1978;
Youth Film Studio of the Beijing Film Institute, founded 1979;
Beijing Children's Film Studio, founded 1981.

Some of them double to produce scientific and educational films, newsreels and documentaries. The Changchun Film Studio also has a dubbing lab to translate and dub foreign films into Chinese.

There are also six specialized film studios in China:
Central Documentary and Newsreel Film Studio in Beijing, founded 1953;
Beijing Scientific and Educational Film Studio, founded 1960;
Shanghai Scientific and Educational Film Studio, founded 1953;
Beijing Agricultural Film Studio, founded 1956;
Shanghai Animated Film Studio, founded 1956, the sole animated film producer in China;
Shanghai Film Translation and Dubbing Studio, founded 1956, which translates and dubs foreign films into Chinese and also translates and dubs Chinese films into English, French, Spanish and Arabic.

Growth of the Film Industry China's film industry was established in the mid-1950s. The Chinese Cinematographic Equipment Company is in charge of the domestic manufacture, allocation and supply of cinematographic equipment, and also of the import of some cinematographic equipment and cinefilm. China has now established a sizeable film industry system with considerable production capacity. By 1980, in addition to the large film machinery plants in Nanjing, Harbin, Shanghai, Beijing and Gansu, there were also 50 film machinery plants and four film manufacturers in other parts of the country. China is now able to produce most of its cinefilm-making equipment, and almost all types of film projectors for use in rural and urban areas. There are more than 10 film processing factories and workshops in the country. The Beijing Film Processing Factory and the Shanghai Cinematographic Factory with their advanced equipment are China's two major film processors. The photosensitive material industry in China is only 20 years old, but is now able to produce a complete range of colour films, black-and-white films and magnetic tapes. But production of cinefilm cannot meet the domestic need in quantity and quality, so a certain amount has to be imported every year.

Film Distribution and Exhibition   The Chinese Film Distribution and Exhibition Company is in charge of national film distribution, publicity and exhibition, and the Chinese Film Export and Import Company is in charge of film import and export. Each province, municipality, autonomous region, prefecture and county has its own film distribution and exhibition company or branch company totalling more than 3,300, and there are film posts at the commune level. These organizations manage cinemas, clubs, projection teams and film distribution in urban and rural areas. Over the past three decades China has gradually established a nationwide film exhibition network. Government policy is to encourage film exhibition by both state-owned facilities and by commune-run facilities. In addition to the construction and expansion of cinemas in the cities, film projection teams have been set up in factories, mines and villages. By the end of 1980, there were 125,000 film projection units in China, of which 83,000 or 67 per cent were in the rural areas, and 41,000 or 33 per cent (including 2,716 cinemas) were in the cities. Before Liberation, China had merely 596 film projection units, mostly in a few big cities and none in the countryside except for the liberated areas.

The supply and maintenance of cinematographic equipment are in the hands of 180 agencies in the provinces, municipalities and autonomous regions, responsible for organizing the manufacture and supply of film projectors and accessories. There are also technical schools or organizations for training film distribution and projection workers. At present, there are 400,000 people engaged in the distribution and showing of films, and the management, supply and maintenance of cinematographic equipment.

(3) FILM EDUCATION AND RESEARCH

The Beijing Film Institute, founded 1956, is the only tertiary-level institution in China for training professional film personnel. It has five departments, directing, acting, cinematography, graphic arts and recording. In the directing department the course lasts for five years and in the other departments for four years.

The Chinese Film Archives, founded 1958, is responsile for collecting, sorting out and preserving copies of Chinese and foreign films and also written and pictorial material. It is a member of the International Federation of Film Archives, and has established exchanges in film data with its counterparts in several countries.

The Film Research Institute of the Chinese Academy of Art, founded 1980, is responsible for research into the basic theories and history of the cinema. It has four sections, on contemporary cinema theory, the history of the cinema, cinema theory and foreign cinema. It publishes the journal *Film and Culture*.

There are also mass research organizations such as the Chinese Film Society, the Chinese Film Criticism Society and the Cinema Arts Society.

The Chinese Institute of Film Science and Technology is responsible for research on film science and technology. It has six groups: acoustics, processing, machinery, architecture, information and translation, and standards. It publishes the bimonthly *International Cinematography*.

(4) THE CHINESE FILM ARTISTS' ASSOCIATION

A mass organization of Chinese film personnel, the Chinese Film Artists' Association is open to all those with achievements in cinematography, film technology, review, education, editing, publishing, archives, enterprise management and organization.

Founded in 1949, it was originally called the National Association of Chinese Film Arts Personnel. It adopted its present name at the Fourth Congress of Literary and Art Personnel in 1979. Its publications include *Popular Cinema*, *Film Art*, *Film Arts Review* and *Film Technology*. The circulation of *Popular Cinema* reaches over eight million copies a month.

The president of the Association is Xia Yan.

(5) EXCHANGE WITH OTHER COUNTRIES

China attaches much importance to the exchange of films with friendly countries and has an extensive film import and export operation. The Chinese Film Export and Import Company has business ties with 180 film distribution firms and agents in 63 countries and regions. China has sponsored an Asian Film Week and exchanged film weeks with many countries. China often sends film delegations to other countries and receives film personnel from abroad. China also sends films and delegations to major international film festivals.

To expand international joint film ventures, China established a National Film Co-production Company in July 1979, for joint filming and providing labour services and assistance in filming with foreign countries on the principle of friendship and mutual benefit. By 1980, it had received some 170 requests by cable or correspondence for joint film ventures, of which 60 were under formal discussion. It has already signed co-production contracts with film companies from Japan, Italy and Canada. In 1980, 18 feature, scientific and educational films and documentaries were made in cooperation with foreign companies, including *Roof Tiles of Tenbyo* and *Beyond Tolerance* (also known as *Real Kung Fu of Shaolin*). Shooting began of the Sino-Italian television film *Marco Polo* and agreement was reached on the production of *The Marvellous Mongolian Horse* in cooperation with the United States, *Norman Bethune* in cooperation with Canada and *The Lady and the Panda* in cooperation with the United States and Hong Kong.

3. FINE ARTS

(1) HISTORICAL BACKGROUND

Primitive Chinese painting can be traced back to the painted pottery of the Neolithic Age, some 6,000 years ago. Those pottery vessels were painted with decorative patterns or representations of human faces, animals and plants. Typical examples are the painted pottery bowls with a pattern of human faces and fish excavated at Banpo near Xi'an, and the painted pottery basin painted with figures of dancers excavated at Datong, Qinghai.

The characteristic art form of the first stages of recorded history in China, from the Shang and Zhou dynasties to the Spring and Autumn and the Warring States periods (c. 16th century B.C. to 221 B.C.), is represented by bronze ritual vessels and other bronze ware, which were often richly decorated. A bronze mirror unearthed at Jixian, Henan, for example, is engraved with a battle scene on land and water which depicts more than 290 figures in hand-to-hand combat, shooting arrows, rowing, beating drums, awarding prizes and bidding farewell. Paintings on silk first appeared during the Warring States Period. The earliest examples discovered so far are two silk paintings from tombs in the state of Chu, one of human figures, dragons and phoenixes, and one of human figures riding dragons. They are in the form of line drawings executed with a hair-tipped brush, the basic technique of traditional Chinese painting.

Wall painting was a development of the Qin and Han dynasties (221 B.C. to A.D. 220). Apart from wall paintings in palaces and temples, there was also a great number in tombs of that period. The earliest Chinese mural so far discovered was in the Han Dynasty tomb of Bu Qianqiu and his wife near Luoyang, Henan. It depicts the buried couple ascending to heaven in the company of immortals and mythical beasts. Han tomb murals have also been found in Henan, Shanxi, Shandong, Hebei, Gansu, Liaoning and Jilin. Sculpture is represented by the life-size pottery soldiers and horses in the tomb of Qin Shi Huang, the first emperor of the Qin Dynasty, and the stone figures lining the approach to the tomb of General Huo Qubing. Both sets of sculptures are extremely lifelike, and each figure is a distinct creation. Of the large quantity of line engravings and low relief carving dating from Han, the most famous are those in the Wuliang Temple in Shandong.

Religious art thrived as never before during the Wei, Jin and Northern and Southern dynasties, from A.D. 220 to A.D. 581. The spread of Buddhism in this period led to the practice of making cliff grottoes and furnishing them with sculptures and wall paintings of Buddhist images. The most famous of these, known the world over, are the Kizil Grottoes in Xinjiang, the Mogao Grottoes at Dunhuang, Gansu, the Yungang Grottoes at Datong, Shanxi, and the Longmen Grottoes at Luoyang, Henan. Construction at the grottoes at Dunhuang began in 366 and continued for more than 1,000 years. Today, 492 caves are still in a fairly good state of preservation, and contain 2,500 painted clay sculptures and 45,000 square metres of murals. The Dunhuang sculptures and murals are outstanding in scale and detail. The most famous of the many noted painters at that time was Gu Kaizhi (c. 345-406), whose graceful, lifelike figures have come down to us today in copied versions of his *Learned Women* and *The Goddess of the Luo River*.

Chinese art reached a new height during the period covered by the Sui, Tang, the Five Dynasties and the Song (581-1279), when the main schools which still dominate traditional Chinese painting were formed. China's earliest-known landscape scroll, *The Spring Outing* by Zhan Ziqian, dates from the Sui Dynasty. Many famous painters emerged during the Tang Dynasty, such as Yan Liben, Yuchi Yizeng, Li Sixun, Wu Daozi and Wang Wei. Wu Daozi was called by his contemporaries "the sage of painting" for his skill in both figures and landscapes. Wang Wei, the inventor of ink-wash landscapes, was also an accomplished poet, and it is said of him that "there is painting in his poems and poetry in his paintings". Landscape painting reached its peak during the Five Dynasties Period and early Song, in the hands of Jing Hao and Dong Yuan (both of the 10th century), and Fan Kuan continued their tradition into the 11th century with his masterpieces *Travellers Along a Mountain Stream* and *Snow-capped Mountains*. Another 10th century painter, Gu Hongzhong, is famous for his depiction of characters in the celebrated *Han Xizai's Night Revels*. The most famous example of genre painting in this period is the Northern Song painter Zhang Zeduan's *Riverside Scene at the Qingming Festival*, a vivid portrayal of the bustling social life of Kaifeng, capital of Northern Song. Grotto sculpture continued to flourish, developing a distinctively Chinese style as it matured. Important examples of funerary statuary are the stone figures leading up to the Qianling (the tomb of the Tang Emperor Gaozong and Empress Wu in Qianxian, Shaanxi), the six horses in bold relief in the Zhaoling, the tomb of the Tang Emperor Taizong (in Liquan, Shaanxi), and the stone sculptures at the seven imperial tombs of the Northern Song Dynasty at Gongxian, Henan.

The Yuan Dynasty (1271-1368) is known for its outstanding ink-wash paintings. During the Ming and Qing dynasties (1368-1911), painting developed along two distinct lines — one, represented by Wang Shimin and Wang Jian, faithfully following the old masters, the other, represented by Xu Wei, Zhu Da and the Yangzhou school, emphasizing the expression of personal feelings. The best-known statuary of this period are the stone figures leading up to the imperial Ming tombs in Nanjing and Beijing. Wood-block printing, first used for printing Buddhist scriptures in the Sui and Tang dynasties, flourished as an art form in the Ming and Qing dynasties. Illustrations for novels, opera scripts and tales of the marvellous, and also New Year pictures by folk artists and albums by professional artists, were all printed from skillfully carved wood-blocks. A further and distinctly Chinese development was ink-wash wood-block printing in several colours. Among the most famous early examples of illustrations made by this method is the Ming *Notepaper from the Ten Bamboo Studio* and the Qing *Mustard Seed Garden Album*.

Twentieth century Chinese art grew up at a time of revolution and was inevitably affected by it. An important turning point was the May 4th Movement of 1919, when the Chinese revolution entered a new era of "blood and fire". The arts of this period were also marked with blood and fire.

The most outstanding achievement in art over the 30 years between the May 4th Movement and the founding of the People's Republic of China was the development of wood-block printing. With the constant support and encouragement of the writer Lu Xun, many fine young engravers produced profound works depicting the miseries of the labouring people and their awakening and rebellion, such as *The Illness* by Li Qun, *The Dockers* by Jiang Feng, *Roar, China!* by Li Hua and *Her Awakening* by Wen Tao.

When the War of Resistance Against Japan broke out in 1937, Chinese artists took an active part in the resistance movement. In the democratic base areas of resistance to Japan, they celebrated whole-heartedly the people's resistance movement, new heroes and new deeds. Outstanding wood-block prints of this period include *Don't Let the Grain Be Seized by the Enemy* by Yan Han, *Settling Accounts with the Landlords* by Gu Yuan, and *Reforming Idlers* by Wang Shikuo.

Notable achievements were also made in the cartoonist's art in this period. The appearance and development of satiric cartoons, in a sense, marks the growth of democratic thinking in a society. In China, satiric sketches first made their appearance in the late Qing Dynasty, and newspaper cartoons developed rapidly in the aftermath of the 1911 Revolution. Foreign cartooning was introduced into China around this time. A cartoonists' association was set up in Shanghai in 1927 and published a weekly called *Shanghai Cartoons*. Many cartoonists expressed their strong sense of responsibility to society by producing cartoons that exposed social injustice, such as Zhang Guangyu's *Song Ziwen Amasses a Fortune*, *Kong Xiangxi Wins a Promotion* and *The Three Fishermen* and Ye Qianyu's cartoon serials *Mr. Wang* and *Young Chen*. Other important cartoonists of the time were Huang Wennong, Shen Bochen, Feng Zikai, Zhang Ding, Ding Cong, Liao Bingxiong, Te Wei, Zhang Leping, Zhang E, Hua Junwu and Cai Ruohong.

Oil painting was first introduced into China from the West in the late 16th century, but its first main period of growth was in the 30 years after the May 4th Movement. Notable oil painters of this period were Liu Haisu, Xu Beihong, Pang Xunqin, Ni Yide, Yan Wenliang and Wang Jiyuan. Xu Beihong's *Tian Heng and His Five Hundred Heroes* and *After Me* were particularly striking.

The creative efforts of Chinese artists before the founding of New China opened up new ground for Chinese art, laid an ideological foundation and prepared the cadre of artists for the development of fine arts in New China.

(2) THE FINE ARTS IN NEW CHINA

Traditional Chinese Painting Traditional Chinese painting began its search for new themes and methods of expression in response to social changes during the 30 years before the founding of the People's Republic. Fruitful initial efforts in this respect were made by Xu Beihong, Gao Jianfu, Chen Shizeng, Qi Baishi, Huang Binhong, Fu Baoshi, Zhao Wangyun and Jiang Zhaohe.

A fundamental change and tremendous progress have been made, however, since 1949. At the First National Exhibition of Traditional Chinese Paintings held in 1953, 240 works by 200 painters were on display. At the second national show in 1956, however, the number of paintings increased to 940, and the exhibitors to 600. In addition to these two national exhibitions, there have also been numerous art exhibitions at the national and provincial level and in army units throughout the country, and traditional Chinese painting has always occupied an important position in such events. Progress is marked not only in the number of works produced, but more importantly, in the breakthrough of limitations in subject-matter imposed since the Yuan Dynasty. Traditional Chinese painting is now no longer just a vehicle for the pleasure of the literati and high officials but has accepted the mission of depicting the lives, struggles and aspirations of the millions of labouring people. Paintings on both modern and traditional themes are now permeated with the spirit of the age. Works which fully deserve the name "new Chinese paintings" include *Testing Mama* by Jiang Yan, *Snowstorm in the Wilderness* by Huang Zhou, *Top-Grade Wool* by Ye Qianyu, *Two Lambs* by Zhou Changgu, *Bringing Food on a Snowy Night* by Yang Zhiguang, *The Water-Sprinkling Festival* by Cheng Shifa, *The Eight Heroines Plunge into the River* by Wang Shenglie, *Revolutionary Storm* by Wu Jingbo and *On Manoeuvres in Northern Shaanxi* by Shi Lu, together with *The People and the Premier* by Lu Chen and Zhou Sicong, which won an award at the 1980 national art exhibition in celebration of the 30th anniversary of the People's Republic, and *Travelling Home* by Liang Changlin and *Do Not Forget Us* by Ji Shu, two prize-winning works from the 1980 national young artists' exhibition. The thoughts and feelings conveyed in these paintings evoke a deep response from the Chinese public. *Snowstorm in the Wilderness*, *Two Lambs* and *Bringing Food on a Snowy Night* have also won international gold medals.

Modern landscape painters continue to study traditional techniques, but also immerse themselves in society and the world around them, opening up new paths and creating their own individual styles through long practice. The most outstanding of the modern period are Huang Binhong, Pan Tianshou, Fu Baoshi, Zhu Qichan, Liu Haisu, Guan Shanyue, Qian Songyan, Li Keran, Li Xiongcai, Zhao Wangyun, Shi Lu, Lu Yanshao and Song Wenzhi.

In bird-and-flower painting, another traditional genre of Chinese art, the emphasis has always been on capturing the likeness of nature to express the artists' sentiments. Modern bird-and-flower painters have carried on this tradition and significant achievements have been made by Qi Baishi, Pan Tianshou, Li Kuchan, Tang Yun, Yu Feian, Wang Xuetao, Chen Banding, Xie Ziliu and Chen Zhifo.

Traditional Chinese painting almost disappeared during the "cultural revolution". After 1976 it began to prosper again, and societies and academies for traditional Chinese painting were restored or founded in provinces and cities. On the national and local levels, the artists' associations have frequently arranged for artists to go to and cities. On the national and local levels, the artists' painting. Painters have carried out research in many directions to improve their work. For instance, the veteran painters Pan Xiezi and Liu Lingcang have pioneered the revival of an almost forgotten style, characterized by fine, delicate brushwork and thickly applied, bright colours, making it shine with a new brilliance. *The Nine Songs*, a combination of traditional Chinese and foreign techniques by the young painter Li Shaowen, is a bold experiment which won its creator a first prize in the Ye Qianyu Awards. The main question for painters of the traditional school today is how to advance traditional painting further and keep it in step with the times.

Oil Painting Chinese oil painters have produced a large number of fine works since 1949 in which Western painting and traditional Chinese aesthetic values have been successfully integrated, such as *The Inaugural Ceremony of the Founding of New China* by Dong Xiwen, *Blood-stained Clothes* by Wang Shikuo, *A Portrait of Qi Baishi* by Wu Zuoren, *Tunnel Warfare* by Luo Gongliu, *The Red Army Crosses Snow-capped Mountains* by Ai Zhongxing, *Comrade Liu Shaoqi with Anyuan Coal Miners* by Hou Yimin, *Liu Hulan's Heroic Death* by Feng

Fasi, *The Five Heroes of Langya Mountain* by Zhan Jianjun, *Woman Committee Member* by Tang Xiaoming, *Criminals on Trial* by Hazi Aimehdi and *Father* by Luo Zhongli. These works have won the admiration of the Chinese people for their profound content perfectly integrated with artistic forms of expression that the great masses of the people can comprehend.

Some oil painters at present are striving to raise in their works social issues of general significance, based on their own actual experience. Examples are *Daring to Give Their Lives* by Li Bin and Chen Yiming, *When We Were Young* by Zhang Hongjun, *Scrapping the Agreement* by Qi Chengxiang and *Father and Son* by Zhu Yiyong. Because these works touch on topics of public concern, they have drawn widespread attention and acclaim. Many young oil painters are also engaged in exploring a wide range of new techniques.

Painting in oils is rapidly increasing in popularity among Chinese artists. At the 1980 national exhibition of paintings by young artists, 50 of the 153 prize-winning works were oil paintings.

Woodcuts Although wood-block printing has a long history in China, the new art of woodcuts only developed in China in the nineteen-thirties in response to Chinese social reality.

After the founding of New China, the older generation of woodcut artists continued to produce many significant works on the new times and new life, such as Li Hua's *Conquering the Yellow River,* Huang Yongyu's *Ashima,* Yan Han's *Qingming Festival 1976,* Wu Biduan's *Lenin and a Chinese Guard,* Gu Yuan's *A Visit to a Former Friend and Comrade-in-Arms,* Li Qun's *After the Commune Cadres' Meeting* and Huang Xinbo's *Lasting*

Youth. The veteran woodcut artist Wang Qi, who continues to produce modern woodcuts, has also made extensive research into the history and theory of traditional Chinese graphic art. A number of younger artists now reaching their maturity, such as Li Huanmin, Wu Junfa, Chen Tianran, Zhao Yannian, Zhao Mei, Xu Kuang, Wu Fan and Wang Gongyi, have already contributed to the development of woodcuts with distinctive and successful work. Wang Gongyi's *Qiu Jin* won a first prize at the national exhibition of works by young artists in 1980.

Sculpture A native Chinese sculpture has been fostered since 1949 in special workshops and studios in Beijing, Shanghai, Shenyang and Guangzhou, and in courses in sculpture departments in art schools and academies.

The Monument to the People's Heroes in the centre of the Tiananmen Square in Beijing is the largest memorial sculpture in China. The monument base is faced with eight scenes from modern Chinese history carved in relief, depicting the great and heroic struggles waged by the Chinese people for national liberation over a period of almost a century.

Other works in similar style since 1949 include *Lu Xun* by Xiao Chuanjiu, *Liu Hulan* by Wang Chaowen, *Mother and Daughter Learning to Read and Write* by Yuan Xiaocen, *Hard Times* by Pan He, *The 10th Anniversary of the Bombing of Hiroshima* by Fu Tianchou, Xiao Chuanjiu and Su Hui, *The Unyielding Arabs* by Fu Tianchou, Liu Xiaoeen and Wang Peng, and two large-scale group sculptures, *The Rent Collection Courtyard* and *The Rage of the Serfs,* both the result of collective efforts.

Some small sculptures of recent years on subjects from ordinary life have also won great popularity. These include *A Dai Girl* by Liu Huanzhang, *Enlightenment* by Zhang Shutan, *The Sound of the Lute* by Zhang Dedi and the animal sculptures of Wang Henei. Chinese sculptors have also made progress in creating new forms and styles. *Responsorial Singing* by Liu Jilin employs the technique of exaggeration, and some sculptors have made use of certain elements from abstract art.

New Year Pictures   The New Year picture is a traditional Chinese folk art particularly popular in the countryside. In the past, New Year pictures were mostly printed from wood-blocks in bright colours, and pasted up around the house every lunar New Year. The most popular subjects included children, fish and fruit (symbolizing abundance and productivity) and mythological figures.

Responding to popular demand, the country's cultural offices and publishing houses have given great attention to the creation and printing of New Year pictures, and sales have been impressive. In 1981, for example, 550 million copies of 1,100 New Year pictures were printed. There have been great changes in the subject-matter of these pictures, which now mainly depict scenes from everyday life, but the ever-popular traditional subjects, for instance from traditional Chinese literature, folktales and mythology, are now being re-issued. New Year pictures from places like Yangliuqing near Tianjin, Taohuawu in Suzhou and Weixian in Shandong, where this particular folk art has been a celebrated tradition for several centuries, have taken on a new life since 1949 and are now sold even on the international market.

Picture Storybooks   Chinese picture storybooks are an indigenous development which bear little resemblance to American comic books. Invariably issued in a small-sized format convenient for portable use, they feature one drawing per page with a caption underneath. Early examples of picture storybooks are clearly derived from the wood-block illustrations for novels and collections of legends, and each book usually related one complete story or episode. The stories themselves were mostly simplified versions of existing novels, either genuine old classics or imitations. The relatively low level of literacy required for following the text plus the extremely popular nature of the material have won these books huge audiences among both children and adults. These huge audiences continue today: between 1976 and 1980, a total of one billion picture storybooks were sold, including 400 million in 1980 alone. The *Picture Storybook Magazine*, which began publication 30 years ago, prints 1.14 million copies per issue.

The artistic level of the illustrations is continually being improved. Some of the illustrators have decades of experience behind them and have attained a very high degree of skill, such as He Youzhi, Liu Jiyou, Hua Sanchuan and Wang Shuhui, while a new generation of illustrators such as Chen Yiming, Liu Yulian and Li Bin have displayed impressive talents. Their collective works *Maples* and *Scars* are technically very advanced and also very moving.

The Chinese Artists' Association sponsored two national awards for picture storybooks, in 1963 and 1981. Among the 77 prize winners in 1981 were *Norman Bethune in China* by Xu Rongchu, Xu Yong, Gu Liantang and Wang Yisheng, *The White Light* by He Youzhi, *Fifteen Strings of Cash* by Wang Hongli, *The White-Haired Girl* by Hua Sanchuan and *Scars* by Chen Yiming, Liu Yulian and Li Bin.

At present there are few picture storybooks on contemporary life. Realizing this, many picture storybook illustrators are striving to overcome this shortcoming and fulfil their duty to society.

Cartoons In 1950, the monthly *Cartoon* was founded in Shanghai, and the First National Exhibition of Cartoons was held in 1956. Despite certain setbacks, the art of the cartoon in New China has continued to flourish, and cartoonists like Hua Junwu, Fang Cheng, Ding Cong, Jiang Yousheng, Ying Tao, Bi Keguan and Liao Bingxiong have been very productive. The one-man show of cartoons by Fang Cheng in the Chinese Art Gallery in 1980 made a great impact. The *People's Daily* features a "Satire and Humour" page once a week, and local and provincial-level newspapers also feature cartoon columns.

(3) EDUCATION AND RESEARCH IN FINE ARTS

There are now seven tertiary-level art academies in China: the Central Academy of Fine Arts, the Lu Xun Academy of Fine Arts, and the fine arts academies of Zhejiang, Guangzhou, Sichuan, Xi'an and Tianjin. There are also departments of fine arts in comprehensive art colleges and teachers' colleges at the provincial, municipal and autonomous region level.

The fine arts academies generally have departments in traditional Chinese painting, oil painting, woodcuts and sculpture. The Central Academy of Fine Arts also has departments in New Year pictures, picture storybooks and art history. The academies enroll both undergraduate and post-graduate students and also run short-term training courses to meet the needs of the many young people who wish to study art.

The major research institutes in fine arts are as follows:

The Institute of Fine Arts, under the Chinese Academy of Art; it includes the traditional Chinese Painting Institute, which is the national centre for the study of traditional Chinese painting.

The Chinese Art Gallery, which has departments of preservation, exhibition and research.

The Beijing Palace Museum, which has a special department for the collection, appraisal, preservation and exhibition of classical Chinese painting. The museum has a permanent historical art treasures exhibition and classical painting exhibition which mounts a permanent display of the paintings of various dynasties. *The Journal of the Palace Museum* devotes generous space to articles on research into classical and modern Chinese painting.

The art museums and historical museums established in other municipalities and at the provincial level have similar tasks. Major institutions include the Shanghai Museum, the Liaoning Museum, the Tianjin Art Museum and the Nanjing Museum.

Chinese artists have set up several societies for the study of fine arts, such as the Society for the Study of Traditional Chinese Painting, the Beijing Society for the Study of Oil Painting, the Society for the Study of Yangzhou School Painting and the Society for the Study of Yangliuqing New Year Pictures. There are also painting academies formed by artists in various parts of the country, such as the Academy of Traditional Chinese Painting, the Beijing Academy of Painting, the Shanghai Academy of Painting and the Shaanxi Academy of Traditional Chinese Painting: these are important centres for the study and practice of painting and other fine arts.

In addition to the department of art history in the Central Academy of Fine Arts, research in art theory is also carried out in the research units in the other tertiary-level fine arts academies.

(4) THE CHINESE ARTISTS' ASSOCIATION

This is a voluntary, mass organization of Chinese artists, open to those who uphold its constitution and whose works have been exhibited, issued or published and have reached a fairly high ideological, artistic or scholarly level, or who have works exhibited in at least three shows organized by the Association or who have made outstanding contributions in organizational work, education, theoretical research, editing, handicrafts or architecture.

The Association was established in 1949 at the First National Congress of Literary and Art Personnel, under the name Chinese Art Personnel Association. It's present name was adopted in 1953 during the Second National Congress of Literary and Art Personnel. The president of the Association up to his death in 1982 was Jiang Feng. The Association publishes two journals, *Fine Arts* and *Fine Arts in China*.

(5) INTERNATIONAL EXCHANGES

China has held 100 art exhibitions in 30 foreign countries since 1949, and has hosted 100 exhibitions of works from 30 countries. Together with other cultural organizations it has also sponsored exhibitions and lectures in commemoration of world cultural figures. In 1980, the Association hosted 27 groups of artists from Japan,

Australia, France, Italy and the United States. In the same year, China sent 14 artists to the Philippines, the United States, Japan and Argentina.

4. HANDICRAFTS

(1) HISTORICAL BACKGROUND

Chinese handicrafts date back to the painted pottery of the Yangshao Culture in the Neolithic Age some 6,000 years ago. Hand-made by women in many different styles, these pots and bowls vividly recorded the settled life of human beings of that time. Their shapes, decoration and the design principles embodied in them are a brilliant jewel in the dawn of Chinese handicraft history. Bronze casting goes back to the Shang Dynasty, more than 3,500 years ago, when the Chinese people's mastery of bronze technology produced vast quantities of exquisite bronzeware. These beautiful, robust examples of ancient metallurgy not only indicate the extravagance of the Shang aristocracy, but are also eloquent testimony to the powerful creativity and native daring of the Chinese people. New developments were also made in jade and bone carving and silk weaving.

The feudal period in Chinese history lasted from the 5th century B.C. to the mid-19th century. During this long period, many different kinds of handicrafts flourished, and fine examples still exist in large quantities of pottery and porcelain, bronzeware, bone and ivory carving, jade carving, weaving, glazing, silk fabrics and embroidery, lacquerware, gold and silver ware, inlaid work and plaster figurines from early times. Although some of these objects were buried underground for thousands of years they are still as perfect as when they were made. Their marvellous workmanship qualifies them as treasures in the cultural history of mankind. Chinese silks, for instance, which reached the old Roman Empire along the Silk Road in the Han and Tang dynasties, have been an important medium in cultural and economic exchange between the East and the West for centuries. Chinese ceramics advanced from pottery to porcelain in the Jin Dynasty, and reached its height during the Song. The world-famous Guan, Ge, Ru, Ding and Jun kilns were founded at this time. The underglaze colour and the soft-glaze three-colours of Tang ceramics gave way to the red-and-green ware and the incised, printed and hand-drawn decorations of Song ceramics, which were replaced in turn by the underglaze red and the blue-and-white porcelain of the Yuan Dynasty and the brilliant colourful glazes of the Ming and Qing dynasties.

From mid-19th century to the founding of New China in 1949, China was a semi-colonial, semi-feudal society. During this period, the native Chinese handicrafts industry suffered serious damage. Some crafts developed in a lopsided fashion while others stagnated, declined or even faced extinction. Nanjing, for instance, an important silk centre during the Ming and Qing dynasties, boasted 50,000 handlooms in 1853, but the number dropped to 5,000 in 1900. The jade carving trade in Beijing occupied 500 households in 1900 but almost none in 1942. The master jade-carver Zhang Yunhe, known as "Bird-carver Zhang" for his jade birds, could not make a living from his skills and was forced to become a rickshaw coolie.

After the founding of New China, the traditional handicraft industry was given close attention and powerful support by the state. In the 1950s, the government implemented the policy of protecting, developing and improving the fine traditions of Chinese handicrafts by granting low-interest loans, supplying raw materials, placing orders, marketing the products, extending the domestic and international market, helping veteran craftsmen resume their old occupations, training apprentices and improving designing. As a result, many handicrafts were saved from extinction and many lost skills were recovered. The old itinerant life or destitution that befell many craftsmen became a thing of the past. Skilled craftsmen were awarded titles such as "Handicraft Artist" and "Handicraft Master" and some were elected deputies to the people's congresses at various levels. The state organized large-scale exhibitions and conferences of skilled craftsmen in 1953, 1957, 1959, 1964, 1972, 1978 and 1980 to encourage the exchange of experience and creative work. A national award exhibition of handicraft arts was held in 1981. Today, there are 2,000 handicraft enterprises in China, employing 300,000 full-time craftsmen and nearly five million part-timers in the urban and rural areas who practise handicrafts as a side line. Some 600 types of articles are in production.

(2) MAJOR HANDICRAFTS

Embroidery Embroidery is a traditional occupation of Chinese women from all ethnic groups and areas of the country. To meet mass demand, much embroidery is now made with modern sewing-machines, though hand-sewn embroidery is still important. There are many different kinds of hand embroidery in China and countless different stitches which produce different effects in texture, tone, shading, bulk and perspective. Besides cottage embroidery in different parts of the country, Chinese embroidery is concentrated in four centres — Suzhou, Guangdong, Hunan and Sichuan, each famous for its particular style.

Drawnwork This is a category of embroidery including network, lace, patchwork, cutwork and woollen embroidery. Drawnwork centres are Chaozhou-Shantou in Guangdong, Yantai in Shandong, Changshu in Jiangsu, Xiaoshan in Zhejiang, Chengdu in Sichuan, Beijing and Shanghai. Products include tablecloths, bed-covers, pillow-cases, curtains, sofa covers, coasters and clothes, and constitute one of China's major exports in a wide international market. Some products have won national awards for excellence, and "ten-thousand-strand" embroidery from Xiaoshan and the Penglaige brand lace from Yantai have won gold medals.

Carpets Pure-wool Chinese carpets made entirely by hand are famous for their excellent quality. They are thick, resilient and feature typical oriental designs, and come in either gorgeous or subdued patterns to suit different surroundings. A special pride of the Chinese carpet industry is the decorative wall-carpet: subjects include human figures, buildings, landscapes, birds, animals and episodes from legends. Beijing, Tianjin, Shaanxi, Xinjiang and Tibet are all renowned carpet centres. Xinjiang and Tibetan carpets incorporate local designs and styles which are very popular on the international market.

Basketry and Matting This craft dates back to even earlier times than pottery. A coloured mat found at a Chu site from the Warring States Period (at Jiangling, Hubei), is badly damaged, but its complicated hook pattern is evidence of an impressive level of skill. Materials used for basketry and matting vary from place to place, mainly bamboo, rattan, coir and palmleaf in the south, and wheat straw and willow twigs in the north. In the countryside both children and adults are skilful at making their own tools, household utensils, hats, food vessels, sandals and toys from these materials. At present there are 500 large-scale basketry enterprises in China and one million part-timers engaged in sideline basketry. Chinese basketware and related goods now occupy 30 per cent of the international market. Some products have won international renown for their practicality and aesthetic value, such as the fine bamboo mats from Shucheng, Anhui, which come in beautiful patterns and can be folded, and the alpine rush mats from Linwu, Hunan, which are soft, light and cool for sleeping on in summer, and can also be folded. The bamboo fans from Zigong, Sichuan, are woven from fine splits of bamboo. A round fan no more than 20 centimetres in diameter has about 1,000 crossings of the fine bamboo splits, and flower-and-bird patterns or landscapes can be woven into the fan. The materials for basketry are mostly uncultivated plants or agricultural by-products such as wheat straw or maize husks and the finished products retain their natural beauty and are also inexpensive. Wheat straw hats from Shandong, willow and chaste-tree articles from Hebei and Henan, *wula* sedge articles from Heilongjiang, *mangji* grass articles from Guangxi, rush, water-plant, rattan and palmleaf articles from Guangdong, "horse-reed" and "dragon's tongue" articles from Fujian, yellow grass articles from Zhejiang, coir articles from Sichuan, assorted bamboo articles from the south and maize husk articles from the north all belong to this category.

Jade and Stone Carving Upper Cave Man in the late Paleolithic Age had already begun to appreciate the decorative quality of jade and other kinds of stone. Cave dwellers selected nice-looking pebbles and bones, carefully drilled a hole through them, threaded them together and hung them around their necks. In the late Neolithic Age, ornaments made from jade, which is much harder than stone, began to appear, such as *bi* (pierced discs), *huang* (pendants), *zhui* (pendants), and beads, which still have an aesthetic appeal today. In the Shang and Zhou dynasties, jade articles were given special social significance, whether as symbols of political authority, ritual objects or symbols of personal morality.

Jade carving (actually jade is too hard to be carved; objects are fashioned by chiselling, grinding, crushing, and boring) in New China today comes in many shapes and sizes. Typical subjects are flowers, birds, animals, pavilions, incense burners, vases, beautiful women from history or legend and other human figures. The carvers' skill is shown in their ability to use the specific character of the raw material to its best advantage, enhancing its beauty and minimizing its flaws. Some masters can even create a large-sized article from a small stone. For example, Zhou Shouhai, a 72-year-old master-carver at the Shanghai Jade Carving Studio, can carve a jade incense burner hung with chains, standing 50 centimetres high without a break, out of a piece of unpolished jade only 16 centimetres high. Wang Shusen, the famous old master-carver in Beijing, is known for his carvings of Bodhidharma (the Buddhist missionary who came to China in A.D. 526), arhats, Guanyin (the Goddess of Mercy), immortals and famous beauties. In 1972 he created the masterpiece "Water-Bladder Agate Cataract", a landscape consisting of an agate mountainside with a semi-transparent waterfall through which a pocket of water trapped inside can be seen. It is a fine example of the carvers' art of exploiting the natural features of the raw material. The Chinese jade industry actually now uses some 30 types of precious stone including white jade (nephrite), jasper, green jade, black jade, jadeite, agate, coral, crystal, sapphire, turquoise and malachite.

Soapstone (steatite) carving is found chiefly in Qingtian, Zhejiang, and Shoushan, Fujian. It comes in three main forms: free-standing figures, relief carving and fretwork. Qingtian and Shoushan carvers are skilled at using the natural colouration of the material to represent the characteristic features of different objects. Qingtian is famous for its "grape mountains", showing rugged cliffs covered with vines from which luscious, ripe grapes hang down. These "grape mountains" are executed in fretwork from natural-colour stone. Shoushan is famous for its flowers, fruits and animals executed in fretwork or as free-standing figures. From a stone 20 centimetres long the Shoushan masters can carve a hen coop containing a score of chickens, each bird a free-standing figure. In Liutang, Hunan, advantage is taken of the local "chrysanthemum" stone (ammonite) to create gorgeous chrysanthemums. This kind of "chrysanthemum carving" has its own distinct position among Chinese handicrafts, and the 92-year-old master Dai Qingsheng won a gold medal at the 1915 Panama International Exhibition with one of his stone chrysanthemums. He began his apprenticeship at the age of 13 and has been creating fine stone carvings for nearly 80 years.

Stone carving is also a part of traditional Chinese architecture. The massive ornamental platforms, terraces, balustrades, arches, columns, lions and so on in old palaces and temples are evidence of the skill of the Chinese working people.

Wood Carving Chinese wood carving was first used as decoration in buildings and furniture, and in feudal times, also for religious purposes. The main categories are boxwood carving, camphorwood carving, longanwood carving, lacquer carving and tree stump carving. Today their use is mainly ornamental, but carved wood is also seen on chests, cabinets and screens. Boxwood trees grow very slowly and the wood resembles ivory with its fine, hard texture and creamy colour. It is suitable for carving human figures. Camphor trees grow extensively in the southern provinces. As the wood has an insect-repellent smell, it is widely used for chests in which clothes are stored, and other furniture. The master wood carver Lou Shuiming, from Dongyang, Zhejiang, has been carving wood for more than 60 years in three Zhejiang towns, Dongyang, Xiaoshan and Hangzhou, and in Shanghai and Hong Kong. The sidetables, coffee tables, dinner tables, chests, wardrobes, sofas and screens he has designed are much sought after by foreign buyers. He works in a traditional bold relief style, creating a marvellous illusion of depth and perspective. Longanwood carving from Fujian is dark but shiny, looking somewhat like metal and with an antique finish. Gold lacquer carving from Guangdong comes mainly in fretwork bold relief. The gold lacquer exterior gives a splendid, opulent appearance to furniture and buildings. The technique is also applied to ornamental objects such as the "gold lacquer crab basket", showing very lifelike crabs crawling on both sides of the basket walls.

Ivory Carving Carving on animal teeth or tusks can be traced to the Stone Age, and carving on whole elephant tusks date back to the Shang Dynasty. The centres of ivory carving in China today are Beijing, Guangzhou and Shanghai. Products include purely ornamental human figures, landscapes, birds, animals, flower baskets, miniature pleasure boats as well as articles of daily use such as chopsticks, face-powder boxes, brooches, seals and mouthpieces of pipes. Beijing is known for its free-standing fugurines; Guangzhou is most famous for its ivory balls, miniature boats and pagodas. Master-carver Weng Rongbiao from Guangzhou is an expert in carving concentric ivory balls. In his father's generation, the greatest achievement was to carve a set of 28 balls from a 10-centimetre piece of ivory, but Weng Rongbiao has perfected his technique so that he can carve 40 or 42 balls from a piece usually big enough only for 26 balls. Recently he set a new record with a carving of 45 concentric balls. Each ball in the set is finely carved and can be independently rotated.

Clay and Dough Modelling A popular folk art in both urban and rural China is modelling animals, heroes from traditional operas and other human figures out of clay or dough. The modellers are mostly peasants who make simple but attractive toys in the slack season to be sold at rural fairs. The colour for the dough figures is mixed in the material in advance, not applied at the end. Though crudely made, these folk toys are much liked for their exaggerated postures and bright colours. This folk art has given rise to a few professional enterprises in different parts of the country, and some research institutes of handicraft arts have sections for clay or dough modelling. The clay and dough figurines of Beijing, Shanghai, Tianjin and Wuxi in Jiangsu are all famous local products. The Beijing dough modeller Cao Yue, the daughter of a famous dough modeller, is carrying forward her father's skills. She can create a scene from *A Dream of Red Mansions* with up to a dozen dough figurines small enough to be put into half a walnut shell. Though only about one centimetre in height, each figure has a lifelike expression and pose.

Lacquer Chinese lacquer is a natural varnish made from the sap of the lacquer tree (*rhus verniciflua*). It dries on exposure to air to form a plastic coat which is resistant to water and acid or alkaline corrosion. It may be applied with or without a colouring agent to a body made of wood, bamboo, leather or metal, or to a frame that is later removed. The lacquer is applied in numerous coats, each of which must be allowed to dry before the next is added. The result is an article which is both practical and beautiful.

The technique of making small lacquer objects was perfected in China by the beginning of the 4th century B.C. and early lacquerware has been found in many archaeological sites throughout the country. Lacquerware today is produced in Beijing, Shanghai, Fuzhou (Fujian), Yangzhou (Jiangsu), Yichun (Jiangxi), Chongqing (Sichuan), Dafang (Guizhou), Pingyao (Shanxi), Tianshui (Gansu) and Yangjiang (Guangdong).

Early lacquerware was mostly restricted to only two colours, black and vermilion. Today's techniques are so advanced that Fujian lacquerware, for instance, not only

is multi-coloured but is combined with gilding, silver and
mother-of-pearl inlay. Beijing lacquerware is based on
the imperial ware of the Ming and Qing dynasties. Up
to 100 layers of lacquer are applied to an object which is
then ready to be finely carved. The end effect is a combination of carving with painting. The Qianlong emperor
(r. 1736-95) had a special fondness for carved lacquer, and
during his reign, the throne, screens and tables were all
carved lacquer; he was buried in a carved lacquer coffin.
Articles of daily use in the palace were also made of
lacquer, from snuff-boxes one inch high to vases more
than a metre high. The main varieties were red lacquer,
yellow lacquer, multi-coloured lacquer and red-and-black
lacquer.

Cloisonne Cloisonne is a kind of enamelware introduced into China in the 14th or 15th century. The
enamel is poured into *cloisons* or compartments formed
by copper wire welded on to an object made of red copper. The enamel is baked on to the object in several
firings, then polished and gilded. The finished article is
a splendid sight with gleaming gilded copper wire separat-
ing each segment of brilliant enamel colour. Cloisonne
trophies for sports competitions embody the lofty value
of the awards.

The principal centre of cloisonne in China is Beijing.
Apart from commemorative and ornamental objects, it
also produces articles for daily use, such as stationery,
smoking accessories, vases, table lamp bases, food con-
tainers, fruit bowls, incense burners, jewelry boxes, mirror frames, folding screens and buttons. One of the major
handicrafts in Beijing, cloisonne production now employs
4,500 workers, compared with only 300 before the founding of New China. Output has also increased several

hundred times. Beijing cloisonne is often presented to distinguished foreign visitors.

(3) TRAINING AND RESEARCH

Handicrafts occupy an important position in the material and cultural lives of the Chinese population, and their widespread use requires a large number of handicraft personnel. The old-fashioned way of handing down skills from father to son or from master to apprentice is far from adequate in satisfying the demands of the present day, and the training of handicraft personnel has to be through schools. However, schools for training handicraft personnel were only set up in the early 20th century. At that time, some art schools had departments of applied arts (some schools had courses on design), but none was on a large scale and there were few teachers and students. Since the founding of New China, along with the rapid development of handicrafts, there has been marked development in both traditional and modern training. There are now at least four academies of fine arts, nine comprehensive arts colleges and seven colleges of light industry which have departments of handicrafts or courses on handicrafts. There are 13 secondary-level arts and crafts schools. The Central College of Arts and Crafts, the first tertiary-level institute of its kind in Chinese history, was established in Beijing in 1956. The college has five departments: dyeing and weaving, ceramics, decorative art, industrial design and speciality handicrafts; and nine majors: dyeing and weaving, fashion design, ceramics, book design, commercial art, interior design, industrial design, book illustration, and ornamental sculpture. Some 2,000 students of handicrafts are enrolled at these colleges and schools, and the staff is continually expanding. (The above does not include handicraft training in normal arts schools, and schools and courses relating to handicrafts established by the economic ministries).

Dozens of research institutes have been set up by the handicraft industry throughout the country. For example, there are ceramic research institutes at Jingdezhen in Jiangxi, Liling in Hunan, Tangshan and Handan in Hebei and Zibo in Shandong. Research institutes for the study of local handicrafts are also established at the provincial or municipal level where centres of these handicrafts exist. These institutes specialize in local handicrafts, learning from and improving the skills of established masters. For example, the Beijing Handicrafts Institute studies jade carving, cloisonne, lacquer and filigree, the Yunjin Institute in Nanjing studies traditional brocade, the Suzhou Embroidery Institute studies traditional embroidery and the Guangdong Handicrafts Institute studies ivory ball carving, Guangdong embroidery and Guangdong-style redwood furniture.

Through foreign trade and exhibitions abroad, Chinese handicrafts have reached more than 100 countries and regions since 1949, increasing foreign understanding of China and promoting friendship. Like the ancient trade in silk along the "Silk Road", the present-day export of Chinese handicrafts will add a new leaf to the cultural history of mankind.

5. MUSIC

(1) HISTORICAL BACKGROUND

China has a long history of musical culture. Documentary evidence and artefacts show a fairly developed musical culture as far back as the Shang and Zhou dynasties. At this time there were slaves whose sole function was to make musical instruments, compose, sing and dance. More than 80 kinds of musical instruments existed during the Spring and Autumn and Warring States periods. The excavation of an early Warring States tomb (of the Marquis of Zeng) in Suixian, Hubei in May 1978 revealed a set of 124 musical instruments, among them a stand of bells (consisting of 64 bells of different sizes and tones and one *bo*, or large hanging bell), a stand of lithophones (consisting of 32 sonorous stones of different sizes and tones), two *guqin* (a kind of lute or zither), one with 5 strings and one with 10 strings, 12 *se* (a kind of zither with 25 strings), one big and one small *chi* (a traverse bamboo flute), two *paixiao* (pan-pipes with 16 pipes), five *sheng* (a set of bamboo pipes) and four drums. This find indicates the enormous scale of orchestras at aristocratic feasts at that time. The neatly-arranged and exquisitely made set of bells is particularly remarkable. Tests have shown that each bell can produce two tones three intervals apart, and altogether they can produce a range of more than five octaves, divided into over 90 musical tones. This is an ample proof of the astonishing level achieved in Chinese music and the manufacture of musical instruments.

Over the many centuries of feudal society, there were many periods during which musical culture flourished. For instance, in the Sui and Tang times there was a golden age when native and foreign music combined to produce a new Chinese music. The chief musical achievement in this period was the development of *daqu*, a kind of musical performance which combined singing, instrumental music and dancing into an integrated whole. The best-known works in this form are *Prince Qin Storms the Enemy Lines*, *Liuyao*, *Yizhou* and *Liangzhou*. The first piece, which consists of 52 stanzas, has an intricate structure and complicated rhythm. The *daqu* orchestra usually consisted of several dozen kinds of musical instruments playing in unison, with attention to contrast and balance in tone colour and volume.

Later, with the rise of opera, the imposing *daqu*, suitable mainly for palace performances, was gradually replaced by the simple but lively opera and ballad music which had popular origins. From the 14th century on, music and singing gained an increasing importance in opera, and there gradually came into being a number of distinctive local opera forms.

The vocal and instrumental music for Chinese opera does not consist of fixed melodies as in the West but of "tune families" or systems. This music, which was not written down, was based on a set of tunes, usually of folk origin, which were open to considerable variation in pitch, melody and rhythm by the performer. Each form of opera is primarily identified by its "tune family", which varies from region to region or even from one locality to another. There were also major advances in music for folk songs and dances, and small ensembles of folk instruments were very active.

Chinese musical culture entered a new period of development after the May 4th Movement in 1919. The spread of the workers' and peasants' movement spurred the development of revolutionary workers' and peasants' songs and produced such revolutionary musicians as Nie Er and Xian Xinghai. Nie Er's "The March of the Volunteers," "Graduation Song" and "Song of the Great Road" and Xian Xinghai's "Go to the Enemy Rear", "On the Taihang Mountains" and *The Yellow River Cantata* hoisted a glorious banner for the growth of proletarian revolutionary music in China.

After 1942, a large-scale campaign to develop *yangge* (a popular folk dance in the north) and modern opera (i.e. a new form of opera closer to Western opera than traditional Chinese opera) was launched in the revolutionary base areas under the leadership of the Chinese Communist Party. Large numbers of musicians enthusiastically went to work in the front-line of the struggle of the workers, peasants and soldiers, creating many *yangge* operas (i.e. operas based on popular *yangge* tunes) such as *Brother and Sister Reclaim the Wasteland*, modern operas such as *The White-Haired Girl* and a variety of excellent popular songs such as "Nanniwan", "Song of Liberation", "Two Little Cowherds", "Girls of the Shanxi-Qahar-Hebei Border Region", "Unity Is Strength", "Without the Communist Party There Would Be No New China", "We Are Democratic Youth" and "We Workers Are Powerful".

(2) **THE DEVELOPMENT OF MUSIC IN NEW CHINA**

After the establishment of New China, musical culture developed on a scale and at a speed unprecedented in

Chinese history. Marked progress was also made in musical education, composition and performance.

Musical Education Over the past three decades the people's government appointed experienced musicians such as Lü Ji, He Lüting, Zhao Feng, Miao Tianrui, Li Jiefu, Chang Sumin, Liu Hengzhi, Li Ling, Ding Shande, Jiang Dingxian, Yu Yixuan, An Bo, Ma Ke, Tan Shuzhen, Zhou Xiaoyan, Zhang Xiaohu and Jiang Fengzhi, to set up eight conservatories of music with attached primary and secondary schools in Beijing, Shanghai, Shenyang, Chengdu, Tianjin, Xi'an and Guangzhou, forming a comprehensive system of musical education from the primary to the tertiary level. These conservatories have departments of composition, folk music, vocal music, orchestral music and the piano. The Central Conservatory of Music and the Shanghai Conservatory of Music also have departments on conducting, musicology, and modern opera and run advanced in-service training courses. Post-graduate classes and opportunities for study abroad are also offered to talented young and middle-aged professional musicians. The eight conservatories alone have more than 1,300 experienced professors, lecturers and junior instructors, and their graduates of the past three decades can be found in all parts of the country; some have already become professional cadres and leading performers in provincial and national professional musical organizations. Most of the young musicians who have achieved outstanding results in national and international competitions have been trained by the staff of these schools directly or indirectly. Departments and courses on music can also be found in the Academy of Art of the Chinese People's Liberation Army, the Central Institute for Nationalities and in Wuhan, Nanjing, Jinan, Changchun and Kunming, and also in teacher training colleges and schools in nearly every province and municipality and in some of the prefectures. These departments and courses also have many experienced professors and young and middle-aged teachers, and over the last 30 years have trained a large number of professional musicians and primary and secondary school music teachers.

Performance Since 1949, the government has allocated huge sums of money and assigned large numbers of people to set up some 40 professional performing arts bodies such as the Central Philharmonic Society; the Central Song and Dance Ensemble; the Central Chinese Music Ensemble; the Oriental Song and Dance Ensemble; the Central Nationalities Song and Dance Ensemble; the Central Modern Opera Theatre; the Chinese Modern Opera and Dance Drama Theatre; the Central Ballet Troupe; the Military Band, Opera Troupe and Song and Dance Ensemble of the General Political Department of the People's Liberation Army; the Chinese Music Ensemble, Orchestra and Choir of the Central Broadcasting Arts Troupe; the Shanghai Modern Opera Theatre; the Shanghai Symphony Orchestra; and the Guangzhou Orchestra. There are also many medium-scale, comprehensive song and dance ensembles at the provincial level. These organizations have many noted conductors, such as Li Delun, Huang Yijun, Yan Liangkun, Han Zhongjie and Zheng Xiaoying; composers such as Li Huanzhi, Liu Zhi, Qu Xixian, Qu Wei, Zhu Qianer, Zhang Rui, Zheng Qiufeng, Wang Ming and Shi Guangnan; instrumental soloists such as Lu Chunling, Liu Dehai, Liu Mingyuan, Wang Guotong, Liu Shikun, Yin Chengzong and Sheng Zhongguo; vocal soloists such as Zhang Quan, Wei Qixian, Hu Songhua, Zhang Yuenan, Wang Kun, Guo

Lanying, Cedain Zhoima and Li Guyi, and over 20,000 other performers. In recent years, many new stars have come to the fore, especially in instrumental music. On the whole, the present kind of training produces large numbers of performers (especially in vocal music) fairly rapidly, but problems still exist in regard to quality, where the training is not strict or comprehensive enough.

Composition Progress in the performing arts has greatly stimulated all types of musical composition. An astonishing number of works has been produced over the past three decades (especially short songs and instrumental pieces), some of them having a considerable impact on the masses. They include the modern operas *Xiao Erhei's Marriage*, *Song of the Grassland*, *The Red Guards of Lake Honghu*, *The Red Coral*, *Ayikuli*, *Sister Jiang*, *Sun Valley*, *Third Sister Liu*, *Red Clouds* and *Regret for the Past*; the violin concerto *Liang Shanbo and Zhu Yingtai*; the symphonic poem *Gadameilin*; the symphonies *The Long March* and *The Qingming Memorial Ceremony*; the orchestra ensemble *The Moon Reflected in the Twin Ponds*; the piano concerto *Mountain Forest*; the cantatas *The Red Army Base Area* and *Ode to the Motherland*; the song suite *The Red Army Fears Not the Trials of Distant March*; the *erhu* solos *Ballads of Northern Henan* and *River Waters*; the *pipa* solo *Dance of the Yi Nationality*; the piano solos *Five Folk Songs of Northern Shaanxi*, *Spring Moonlight and Flowers on the River*, *Twin Butterfly Variations* and *Children's Suite*; the violin solos *The Sun Shines on Tashkergan*, *Honghe Folk Songs* and *Spring in Xinjiang*; and the popular and lyric songs "Sing the Praises of Our Motherland", "Pass on Lei Feng's Rifle", "We Are Marching on the Great Road", "Unite, Workers of All Countries", "The Sun Never Sets on the

Grasslands", "My Country", "Slow Down, My Horse", "A Toast" and "Allow Me, Please".

Traditional Chinese Music Since Liberation, the people's government has allocated a great deal of manpower and material for the investigation of the vast realm of traditional Chinese music. The Ministry of Culture, acting in cooperation with the Chinese Musicians' Association and provincial cultural departments, has made two large-scale surveys and collections of folk songs, and preparations are under way to compile an enormous collection of Chinese folk songs in about 30 volumes, which will include musical scores and records. Units in the provinces, municipalities and autonomous regions have also made surveys of local types of operas and music, and have also given necessary support to the development of existing local operas and music and promoted their gradual reform. For instance, new genres of traditional opera, such as Beijing Quju and Guangxi Caidiaoju, Yingdiaoju and Jilin Opera have been created; old operas such as Kunqu, Yiyang Opera, Liyuan Opera, Puxian Opera, Gaojia Opera, Tibetan Opera, Zhuang Opera, Plum Blossom Drum Opera and Nanying have been revived and reformed; local operas such as Pingju, Shaoxing Opera, Xiju, Huangmei Opera and Lüju have been enriched and raised to a higher level, and modern themes have been encouraged in traditional genres such as Beijing Opera, Shaanxi Opera and Flower-Drum Opera.

The reform of traditional Chinese music also includes reform and new inventions in the manufacture, content and music of traditional musical instruments. In the past three decades, reforms have been made to the *yangqin* (a dulcimer with metal strings, played with two light slips of bamboo), the *guqin* (a seven-stringed plucked instrument), the *zheng* (a 21- or 25-stringed zither), the *erhu* (a two-stringed fiddle), the *di* (a bamboo flute, blown traversely), the *sheng* (a set of bamboo pipes), the *Lusheng* (reed *sheng*) and other instruments, enlarging their range, improving their tonal colour and enriching their sound. Special efforts have been made to improve and trial-produce bass instruments, which are rather weak. Ensembles for performing traditional music have been formed, such as the Central Broadcasting Arts Troupe, the Central Documentary and Newsreel Studio Orchestra, the Central Chinese Music Ensemble and the Chinese Music Ensemble of the Jinan P.L.A. Vanguard Song and Dance Troupe, and extraordinarily large numbers of new works have been written for solo or ensemble performance. These reforms are designed to make this traditional art form, which is loved and appreciated by the masses, reflect the new realities more vividly and profoundly and bear stronger and clearer contemporary character in musical vocabulary, style, presentation and performing techniques.

Theoretical Research Before 1949, research in music theory in China was basically in a state of total neglect. There were no musicology research institutes in the country nor any musicological research groups apart from a small number of musicologists working on their own. The Music Research Institute of the Chinese Academy of Arts was founded five years after Liberation, and a musicology department was added to the Central Conservatory of Music in 1957. Musicological sections were also attached to the Shenyang Conservatory of Music, the Shanghai Conservatory of Music, and the Hubei Arts Institute. The Chinese Musicians' Association and the Central Conservatory of Music publish theoretical journals on music such as *People's Music, Music Research, Journal of the Central Conservatory of Music, Chinese Music* and *The Art of Music*. A corps of professional musicologists has emerged to lay the foundation for the future development of musicology. Several mass organizations engaged in the presentation and research into folk music have been set up or revived in Beijing, Shanghai and other places, such as the Beijing Society for Research on the *Guqin* and the Jinyu Society for Research on the *Guqin* in Shanghai. Under the sponsorship and promotion of these bodies, extensive efforts have been made to investigate, record and re-edit traditional Chinese music and compile important documentary collections such as *A Complete Collection of Music for the "Qin", A Collection of "Guqin" Music, New Scores of Thirteen "Pipa" Melodies of the Southern and Northern Schools* and *Thirteen Sets of String Instrumental Music* plus collections of research materials such as *Guangzhou Music* and *Wind and Percussion Music of Southern Jiangsu*. Organizations for the arts have also conducted many general surveys of the music of China's ethnic minorities. Certain important works of ethnic minority music, such as the Uygur *Twelve Mukams* and the Dong *Dage* have been examined and re-edited. The Chinese Musicians' Association, the Music Research Institute, the Central Conservatory of Music and the Shanghai Conservatory of Music have organized specialists and teachers to carry out research and compile teaching materials on the history of music in ancient, modern and contemporary China, various kinds of traditional Chinese music, and valuable documents on music found during archaeological excavations.

(3) THE CHINESE MUSICIANS' ASSOCIATION

This is a voluntary, mass organization of Chinese musicians, open to all Chinese composers, performers, musicologists, educators, librettists, editors, translators, and organizers who support the Association's regulations and whose works, performances and work have been widely recognized.

Originally known as the National Association of Chinese Music Personnel, it was founded at the First National Congress of Literary and Art Personnel in 1949 and took its present name in 1959. The Association publishes the journals *People's Music, Songs* and *Librettos*. The president of the Association is Lü Ji.

(4) EXCHANGES WITH OTHER COUNTRIES

Never before has China attained such a scale in the exchange of musical culture with other countries as today. Since the 1950s, Chinese musicians have participated in a wide variety of international music contests in which a number of young talents such as Liu Shikun, Gu Shengying, Yin Chengzong, Li Mingqiang and Hu Kun have achieved excellent results. Many world-famous musicians such as David Oistrakh, Richter, Yehudi Menuhin and Isaac Stern and orchestras such as the Philadelphia, the Boston Symphony, the Berlin Philharmonic, the Vienna Philharmonic and the Prague Symphony Orchestra have given performance tours in China. In 1980, the Chinese Musicians' Association was formally elected to the International Musicological Society and took part in its related organizations and activities, further strengthening Chinese musicians' ties with their colleagues in other countries.

6. DANCE

(1) HISTORICAL BACKGROUND

Chinese dance has a long and brilliant history. Based on their life of collective labour, people in ancient times created primitive dances mimicking the hunt, battle, sacrifices and love. The earliest depictions of Chinese dance are three drawings on a coloured pottery bowl from the Neolithic Age, excavated in Qinghai. By the Western Zhou, dance had already reached a high level, and full-length dances portraying sacrificial ceremonies were performed at court. Many Han Dynasty figure paintings and pottery figurines excavated after 1949 depict interesting and graceful dances such as the *Seven-Dish Dance* and the *Silk Dance*. Traditional dance reached its peak in the Tang Dynasty, a time when music also flourished. Dances were often accompanied by music, as for instance in the *Hu Xuan Dance*. "Hu" refers to the Western Regions of the Tang empire, including what is now Xinjiang and parts of Central Asia; "xuan" means spinning; the dancers whirl swiftly around and their long silk ribbons, scarves and other ornaments fly gracefully with their movements.

Another dance to music was *Rainbow Skirts and Feathered Robes* popular at court and among officials. The graceful, fairy-like movements of this dance have been praised in many Tang poems. As the Chinese theatre developed in the 13th and 14th centuries, dance gradually merged into opera and became an integral part of opera performance; at the same time dance gradually ceased to exist as an independent art form. However, folk dances were still very popular in the countryside in a wide variety of forms, and some continued to be performed down to modern times.

Modern Western dance was introduced into China after the May 4th Movement of 1919. Pioneers like Wu Xiaobang and Dai Ailian working under difficult conditions devoted themselves to the study and exploration of a native Chinese dance theatre, creating many new dances exposing the dark old society and reflecting the people's revolutionary struggle. Among their works are *By the Huangpu River*, *Shameless Bragging*, a satire on the KMT rule, *Air Raid*, *Song of the Guerrillas* and *Child for Sale*. At the revolutionary bases in Yan'an and other places, folk dances of north China such as *yangge* and the "waist-drum dance" became the basis for new dances to inspire the people in their struggle.

(2) **DANCE IN NEW CHINA**

After the founding of the People's Republic, Chinese dance personnel carried out the policy of "letting a hundred flowers blossom and weeding through the old to bring forth the new" and "making the past serve the present and foreign things serve China". They investigated and re-edited a great number of traditional native and folk dances, and created a new Chinese dance-drama and ballet. Many new dances were composed on themes from Chinese revolutionary history and contemporary life, reaching a fairly high level both in content and artistic form and promoting amateur song and dance performances among the masses. This laid a solid foundation for the development of Chinese dance.

Folk Dance All 56 ethnic groups in China have their own rich and distinctive dance traditions. In the old society, the suppression of ethnic folk dances by reactionary rulers brought many ethnic traditions to the brink of extinction. After Liberation, emergency measures were taken to preserve these valuable legacies. Government cultural offices and the Dancers' Association sent dancers to ethnic minority areas to collect and learn local folk dances. Professional ethnic song and dance troupes were also founded and national and local level performances of folk music and dances were organized. These measures promoted wider circulation and popularization of folk dances. More than 2,000 dance forms were discovered and revised during the period 1949 to 1966. After revision these folk dances took on a brand-new appearance. Retaining traditional folk styles, they also showed the outlook of people in the new society. Among the many excellent ethnic dances are *Lotus Dance* and *Red Silk Dance* (Han), *Ordos* and *Herdsmen's Dance* (Mongolian), *Country Joys Dance* and *Long Drum Dance* (Korean), *Song of the Grasslands* (Tibetan), *Grape-Picking Dance* and *Tambourine Dance* (Uygur), *Peacock Dance* (Dai), *Joyous Yi People* and *Moon Dance* (Yi) and *Happy Miao People* (Miao), which have won praise from audiences in China and abroad.

After 1976 there was a new wave of interest in folk dance. Cultural festivals and performances were held in provinces, municipalities and autonomous regions in 1978, and in 1979, song and dance troupes from Xinjiang, Ningxia, Tibet, Yunnan, Inner Mongolia, Sichuan, Qinghai, Hebei and Jiangsu came to Beijing to give performances in celebration of the 30th anniversary of the founding of the People's Republic of China. A large number of excellent folk dances were staged including the Uygur *Sainaimu at Daolang* ("Sainaimu" is a traditional Uygur melody, Daolang is the name of a place in Xinjiang); *Lantern Display* from Sichuan; the Korean *The Rice Is Ripe* and *The Water Watcher* from Yanbian in Jilin; the Uzbek *Joy Overflows;* the Tu *Meeting the Bride* from Qinghai; and the Mongolian *Camel Bell*. The Ethnic Minorities Theatrical Festival held in 1980 was the largest-scale review of folk music and dance since the founding of New China. Taking part were theatre troupes and ensembles of 55 ethnic groups from 18 provinces, municipalities and autonomous regions. More than 300 items were staged including 140 dances such as the Gaoshan *Pestle Dance,* the Tibetan *Lion Herding Dance,* the Sala *Alima,* the Lisu *Stamping Dance,* the Shui *Bull Fight,* the Bai *White Crane Dance,* the Tajik *Joyful Pamirs,* the Daur *Happy Girls,* the Tu *Larenbu and Qiwensuo* (a wedding dance-drama), the Qiang *Date Flowers Blossom,* the Manchu *Mang Shi* and the Hani *Drum Dance. Happiness on Distribution Day,* a Korean dance based on real life, was boldly inventive in theme and choreography, raising new questions in regard to continuing and developing traditional folk dance.

Native Dance-Drama Small-scale dance-dramas and operas with a strong dance element have been preserved in traditional folk dances and opera. In the early years after the founding of the People's Republic, Chinese dance personnel created a few dance-dramas on historical and contemporary themes, drawing on techniques from dances in traditional opera and from folk dance, and applying traditional ways of characterization. Productions of this type, such as *Master Dongguo* and *Stealing Magic Herbs*, laid the foundations for creating a native Chinese school of dance-drama. The folk opera and dance-drama group of the Central Experimental Modern Opera Theatre was formally organized into China's first dance-drama troupe in 1954, and later divided to form the Chinese Modern Opera and Dance-Drama Theatre and the Central Modern Opera Theatre. The former is now responsible for the creation and performance of native Chinese dance-drama and modern opera. The Shanghai Modern Opera and Dance-Drama Theatre and other local song and dance troupes are also engaged in work on Chinese dance-drama. By 1966, a native dance-drama theatre with a distinctive Chinese style had been built on this foundation and the experience of foreign works. Among the successful achievements of this period were several works on modern themes, such as *Five Red Clouds*, *The Xiangjiang Flows North* and *The Red Detachment of Women*. Even more successful were *The Magic Lotus Lantern*, a fairy tale, and *The Small Dagger Society*, on a peasant uprising in the last years of the Qing Dynasty. Working under extremely difficult conditions during the "cultural revolution", dance personnel still managed to present *The Rent Collection Courtyard* and *The White-Haired Girl* as dance-drama.

After 1976, native dance-drama entered a prosperous period in which it has reached a new level of artistry. Excellent works in recent years include *Along the Silk Road*, composed by the Gansu Song and Dance Troupe, about the friendship between Chinese and foreigners in the Tang Dynasty; *Princess Wencheng*, by the Chinese Modern Opera and Dance-Drama Theatre, a historical tale set in the Tang Dynasty; *Cleft Mountain* and *Flight to the Moon*, two fairy tales by the Shanghai Modern Opera and Dance-Drama Theatre; *Zhaoshutun and Nanmunuona* by the Yunnan Song and Dance Troupe, a popular legend from the Dai people (Zhaoshutun is a prince and Nanmunuona a princess from the peacock kingdom); *Going out to Battle*, by the Qinghai Song and Dance Troupe and based on *Gesser Khan*, a Tibetan folk epic about a legendary hero; and *Golden Phoenix*, by the Nanjing Front-line Song and Dance Troupe, on a modern theme. Of all these, *Along the Silk Road* has had the greatest impact. It tells the story of an old master painter in the Dunhuang Grottoes and his daughter, who save a Persian merchant from a sandstorm in the Gobi Desert. Based on the dance movements portrayed in the Dunhuang cave murals, it recreates the elegant and graceful style of Tang dancing which had been lost for centuries.

Ballet Studying foreign dance for Chinese use has been an important policy since the founding of New China. In order to learn from and introduce to China foreign dance to enrich the Chinese people's cultural life, the Chinese government invited foreign ballet teachers to start a ballet class for advanced studies at the Beijing School of Dancing in 1954. The Experimental Ballet Company of the Beijing School of Dancing, the first ballet company in China, was formed in 1959, and within a few years, performed famous European classical ballets such as *Swan Lake*, *The Fountain of Bakhchisaray* and *The Corsair*. The first ballet dancers received their training through actual performance. Ballet personnel then went on to transform foreign classical ballet into a revolutionized and sinicized dance form. Retaining the original character of ballet, they drew on traditional Chinese dance and made further innovations, thus creating a new type of ballet which depicts the Chinese people's life in a truly native style. The first fruits of these endeavours were *The Red Detachment of Women* and *The White-Haired Girl*, both on modern themes. During the "cultural revolution", Jiang Qing and her associates completely banned traditional classical ballet, and misappropriated for their own purposes *The Red Detachment of Women* and *The White-Haired Girl*. After Jiang Qing's counter-revolutionary clique was smashed in 1976, *Swan Lake*, *The Corsair* and other classical ballets were performed again, as well as *Coppelia*, *The Little Mermaid* (transformed into a Chinese fairy tale) and *Rose*, a real-life drama. In 1979, the Beijing Dance Academy successfully re-edited and performed Hans Christian Andersen's fairy tale *The Match Girl*. In 1980, the Shanghai Ballet Company scored an artistic success with its choreography and performance of *The Soul*, based on Lu Xun's short story "The New Year's Sacrifice".

Modern Dance After the founding of New China, the people's government encouraged dance personnel to plunge into the thick of life and integrate with the masses of people, thus opening up a new realm for dance choreography. A great number of dances on historical and contemporary themes were created in the 17 years before the "cultural revolution", such as *Long Live the Victory of the People* and *Great Unity Among All Chinese*, on the great victory won by the revolutionary people; *Luo Shengjiao*, *A Thousand Miles of Lovely Land* and *Song of the Volunteers*, on the militant friendship between the

Chinese and Korean people in the War to Resist U.S. Aggression and Aid Korea; *The Five Heroes of Mt. Langya, Years of Hardship, Storming Luting Bridge* and *March of the Swords*, on themes from revolutionary history; *On the Road to Camp for Field Training* and *Laundry Song*, about life in the People's Liberation Army and relations between the army and the people. These and shorter items have all been well received by audiences. After the "cultural revolution", choreographers, directors and dancers emancipated their thinking, enlarging the range of subjects and techniques for expressing modern life in dance. Innovations were encouraged in theme, genre, form and style. At the 1980 national dance contest for solo, pas de deux and trio performances, great breakthroughs were made in regard to theme, genre and style in works such as *War Drums on Gold Mountain, Goodbye, Mama, Hope, Ah! Tomorrow, Little Radish, Water* and *Song Without Words*. Among the 206 items performed, 120 were on modern themes; not only was this a comparatively high proportion, but the artistic quality was also quite high. The same occasion also saw an increase in the number of dances using flowers, birds, fish, insects and other natural phenomena to express thoughts and feelings and to praise lofty sentiments, such as *Spring Silkworm*, about people who devote their whole lives to serving the masses, *Little Golden Deer*, which celebrates youthful vigour, *Petrel* and *The Scholar and the Fairy Carp*. *War Drums on Gold Mountain* and *The Drunken Sword* are both on historical themes, *The Surprising Transformation* is based on the famous legend *The White Snake* and *The Farmer and the Snake* is from a well-known fable. In all of these works, the emphasis is on character portrayal and the depiction of the characters' inner worlds. A wide range of old, modern, Chinese and foreign techniques were drawn on and amalgamated to form original new types of dance. To sum up, the appearance of these works marks considerable progress in the development of modern Chinese dance.

Folk Dance It is an age-old custom on traditional holidays in China for people to watch or even to take part in folk dancing in the streets or squares. Such open-air performances do not need stages or a large number of props, and the free and easy atmosphere encourages mass participation. In the Haicheng region of southern Liaoning there are more than 300 new *yangge* groups involving 50 per cent of production brigades, and during the Spring Festival in northern Shaanxi, dozens of villages usually get together to put on combined *yangge* performances. Folk dancing is even more popular and lively in the ethnic minority regions, where men and women, old and young, sing and dance throughout the night on holidays and other festive occasions. Mass folk dancing is particularly colourful and occurs in many different forms across the country. There are no less than 100 such dances among the 23 ethnic groups in Yunnan. The Han *yangge* vary greatly from region to region, but are found mostly in the north, whereas the Han lion dance and dragon dance are popular across the country. However, because of differences in customs and habits between north and south China, these dances tend to be rather bold and robust in the north and more delicate and subject to more variation in the south. After the founding of New China, most traditional folk dances incorporated material depicting life in the new society. At the Spring Festival or on national holidays over the past few years, people of all ethnic groups have spontaneously held grand mass song and dance festivals, such as the *yangge* festival held during the 1980 Spring Festival in the Huimin region of Shandong, where out of 996 villages in one county 950 took part. At the 1980 Spring Festival *yangge* fair in Miyun County, Beijing, over 60 dances were performed, such as the land boat (with a model boat used as a stage prop), the *Flying Trident Dance*, walking on stilts, the *Lion Dance*, the *Dragon Dance*, the *Waist-Drum Dance*, the *Red Silk Dance* and the *Big-Headed Baby Dance*. Both traditional and modern themes were featured at these festivals.

The development of amateur folk dancing among the masses has enriched people's cultural and recreational life, and also provided abundant material for stage presentations of folk dancing.

(3) EDUCATION AND RESEARCH

The Beijing Dance Academy is the only tertiary-level dance school in China at present. Originally established as the Beijing School of Dancing in 1954, it assumed its present form in 1979. The academy consists of an undergraduate college and a secondary school. Within the college is a department of education, which has two divisions, one of Chinese classical dance and one of Chinese folk dance, each lasting for four years. Departments for directing, performing and theory are planned for the future. The secondary school has courses on Chinese dance and ballet, and enrolls pupils for six years from the fourth and fifth grades of primary school. The school has its own experimental ballet company.

There are three other secondary-level professional dance schools, the Shanghai School of Dancing, the Guangzhou School of Dancing and the Sichuan School of Dancing.

The Central Institute for Nationalities, the Academy of Art of the People's Liberation Army and other arts institutes and schools all have courses or classes in dancing. The dance class at the Central Institute for Nationalities, established in 1957, which was among the earliest, was converted into a dance concentration in 1959. This Institute has made definite contributions to the training of ethnic minority dancers.

Classes on training, advanced studies and research formed an important part of dance education in the early years after the founding of the People's Republic, and are still conducted throughout the country.

The Dance Institute under the Chinese Academy of Art, the Children's Song and Dance Society of China and other mass research organizations are responsible for the theoretical study of dance in China.

(4) THE CHINESE DANCERS' ASSOCIATION

The Chinese Dancers' Association is a national, voluntary, mass organization of dancers. It is open to all who are engaged in dance choreography, performing, teaching, research, editing, composing, design or organization and who have reached a certain level of achievement, along with folk dancers and mass activists whose work is well-known in their ethnic groups or localities, and who approve of its rules and regulations.

Founded in 1949, the Association was initially known as the National Association of Chinese Dance Personnel;

its present name was adopted in 1979. The Association publishes *Dance*, a series on dance and other publications. Its president is Wu Xiaobang.

(5) EXCHANGES BETWEEN CHINA AND FOREIGN COUNTRIES

Since 1949, many excellent Chinese dances have gained considerable international fame. A dozen prizes have been won over the years at the World Youth Festivals. The Oriental Song and Dance Ensemble was founded to promote mutual understanding and friendship between the Chinese people and people of other countries, performing Asian, African and Latin American songs and dances to enthusiastic receptions in and outside China. There is also a Chinese ballet troupe which performs European ballet for Chinese audiences. With the development of international exchanges in recent years, the number and range of exchanges in dance have increased. Many song and dance troupes and well-known individual performers from Britain, Canada, the United States, Spain, Mexico, Korea, New Zealand, Pakistan, Sri Lanka, West Germany, Japan, India, Egypt and Sweden have toured China, bringing with them a wide range of forms and schools of dancing. Many noted foreign dancers have been invited to teach or work in China. China has also sent many dance troupes or art ensembles including dancers to tour Asian, African and Latin American countries. Chinese delegations have taken part in international ballet performances for fellow-professionals in Japan and the United States and international contests. China was represented at the UNESCO International Council in 1980 by Dai Ailian.

7. QUYI

(1) HISTORICAL BACKGROUND

Quyi is a general term that covers several different types of performances where speech, singing or both are used to relate a story, portray characters, convey feelings and ideas and reflect social life. The many different forms of *quyi* are all simple and convenient to stage and easy to understand. Performances consist usually of only one or two people, there is a minimum of stage props, and no stage scenery. A solo singer or speaker may take several different roles in one performance, and first-person commentary often accompanies narrative. Except for *xiangsheng*, a kind of comic monologue or dialogue, most *quyi* have some kind of musical accompaniment. Clappers (a kind of castanets) are popular in north China, and small drums in central and south China. One performer might sing or recite to the accompaniment of another, or a solo performer might sing or speak and play an instrument such as clappers at the same time. Both men and women can be performers, soloists or accompanists.

Quyi is among China's oldest performing arts; "performers" are mentioned in records that go back over 2,000 years, and figurines of "reciters" have been unearthed from a Han Dynasty tomb in Chengdu, Sichuan. In the long period under feudalism, the development of commerce and handicrafts and the growth of cities brought about the appearance of popular entertainment areas in the cities where popular entertainments flourished. Today there are over 300 different forms of *quyi* in China. Some are spoken, such as *xiangsheng*, *pinghua* and *pingshu*;

some are sung, such as *danxian*, *jingyun dagu* and *qinshu*; some combine singing with speech such as Suzhou *pingtan* and *xihe dagu*; some are half sung and half spoken such as *kuaiban* and *kuaishu*. Some tell long stories which continue over several months; others are short pieces that can be finished in a few minutes or even in a few lines.

Quyi has been created by working people and folk artists; it has a broad mass basis and a strongly Chinese flavour. Many items reflect to a certain degree the aspirations of working people and thus have been favoured by the great masses of the people. However, in the course of circulating over a long period of time, they have inevitably been tainted by feudal thinking.

Quyi performances were despised by the ruling classes in the old society and were not allowed on grand occasions. The performers occupied a low social position, and many earned their living in the streets like beggars. For this reason, *quyi* was facing extinction on the eve of the founding of New China.

(2) THE REVIVAL OF QUYI

The founding of New China brought new life to *quyi*. The ranks of *quyi* performers grew and their social position rose considerably. *Quyi* performers have been elected to the National People's Congress, the Chinese People's Political Consultative Conference and the people's congresses and the CPPCC at local levels. A large number of amateur *quyi* performers have emerged in all walks of life, and their compositions and performances have greatly enriched people's cultural life. These amateurs are also a source of fine new talent for the ranks of professionals.

Reforms to Traditional Quyi Much work was done in the 17 years between 1949 and 1966 in collecting, compiling and revising traditional *quyi* in the spirit of critically adopting China's cultural heritage. The traditional repertoires of established performers were recorded and edited, such as Wang Shaotang's *Outlaws of the March* (Yangzhou *pinghua*), Chen Shihe's *Strange Tales of Liaozhai* (*pingshu*), Zhang Shouchen's *The Little Fairy* and *The Wax Melting Pin* (*xiangsheng* monologues), Ma Liandeng's *The Generals of the Yang Family* (*pingshu*) and Gao Yuanjun's *Story of Wu Song* (Shandong *kuaishu*). The most popular forms of *quyi* in each locality were also collected and edited. For example, cultural offices in provinces and cities like Liaoning and Xi'an have collected and published in book form large numbers of shorter items. These efforts have helped enrich the *quyi* repertory and preserve much valuable material.

New Works (1949-1966) Inspired by the great victories of the Chinese revolution and socialist construction, *quyi* performers composed many new works in the first 17 years after Liberation, joined in some instances by poets and writers. The large number of successful works in each genre and from all parts of the country include *A Cartload of Sorghum* (Shandong *kuaishu*), *Storming the Luding Bridge* (*changci*), *Marriage and Superstition* and *Buying Monkeys* (*xiangsheng*), *The Zhou Detachment Creates Trouble in Pingchuan* and *Tempered in Flames* (*pingshu*), *The Home of Soldiers* and *Learning from Lei Feng* (*Shulaibao* and *kuaibanshu*), and *Dielianhua* (*pingtan*) on a poem by Mao Zedong. Some performers and writers adapted novels, dramas and film stories such as *The Song of Youth, Tracks in the Snowy Forest* and *Li Shuangshuang* for *quyi* performance, and historical stories, fairy tales and legends were also rewritten for the *quyi* repertoire.

The expression of new content required changes in form and this has resulted in a new development in *quyi* techniques. For instance, *shulaibao*, a kind of clapper ballad, has developed from a simple impromptu performance inspired by a single, immediate event into today's *kuaibanshu*, a form that can skilfully relate complex plots and portray characters very vividly. Suzhou *pingtan*, a form of ballad singing accompanied by a three-stringed guitar, was sung in a sentimental, graceful style, but now it can be sung in a bolder and more heroic style. New forms of *quyi* also emerged during this period such as Tianjin *kuaiban*.

The Revival and New Development of Quyi in Recent Years *Quyi* suffered untold damage during the "cultural revolution". Most *quyi* troupes were disbanded and many good items in the *quyi* repertory were repudiated as "poisonous weeds". After 1976, rapid progress was made in the revival of *quyi*. The Association of Chinese *Quyi* Personnel was restored, along with its provincial, municipal and regional branches, and many troupes which were disbanded have regrouped. In the past four years, many excellent new works have appeared all over the country. *Xiangsheng*, a kind of monologue or dialogue which is by nature highly satiric, for instance, played a particularly militant role in criticizing Lin Biao and Jiang Qing, and items such as *The Label Factory, A Peculiar Life, Taking Photos* and *Braggarts* were received with great enthusiasm. Many new items in praise of the old generation of proletarian revolutionaries and new figures and new ethics in the modernization drive have also won praise. Good items written or re-edited during the first 17 years after the founding of New China have been gradually been revived on stage.

At present, there are about 100,000 *quyi* performers in China. *Quyi* troupes and teams have been established in each province, municipality and autonomous region and also in many prefectures and counties, such as the Central Broadcasting Recitation and Ballad Troupe, the Beijing *Quyi* Troupe, the Shanghai *Pingtan* Troupe, the Tianjin *Quyi* Troupe, the Jiangsu *Quyi* Troupe, the Suzhou *Pingtan* Troupe, the Zhejiang *Quyi* Troupe, the Shenyang *Quyi* Troupe and the Sichuan *Quyi* Troupe. There are also many professional *quyi* troupes and groups in the PLA, as well as a large number of amateur *quyi* groups.

An Institute for Research on *Quyi* has been established under the Chinese Academy of Art, and research is also organized by the Chinese *Quyi* Artists' Association and its local branches.

(3) THE CHINESE QUYI ARTISTS' ASSOCIATION

This is a voluntary, mass organization of *quyi* artists, including composers, performers, musicians, reseachers, educators, editors and organizers. It carries out its own training programmes and promotes activities such as composition, performance, reform, research and international cultural exchange.

Its predecessor was the Chinese National Association for Reform in *Quyi*, founded in 1949. In 1953, the Association of Chinese *Quyi* Personnel was formally inaugurated. The present name was adopted during the Fourth National Congress of Literary and Art Personnel in 1979. The Association publishes the journal *Quyi*. Its president is Tao Dun.

8. VARIETY ARTS: ACROBATICS, JUGGLING, CONJURING AND CIRCUS ARTS

(1) HISTORICAL BACKGROUND

Chinese variety arts had already become an independent and highly skilled art form 2,000 years ago. Han Dynasty variety programmes included items such as tight rope walking, handstands, tripod lifting, pole climbing, ball jumping and sword jumping, along with conjuring tricks such as legerdemain, knife swallowing and fire eating. These variety acts are vividly depicted in tomb wall paintings, painted bricks, stone engravings and pottery figurines belonging to the Han Dynasty excavated in recent years in Shandong, Sichuan, Henan, Liaoning and Inner Mongolia.

Progress in Chinese variety arts was very great during the Tang Dynasty, between the 7th and 10th centuries, when performances were often held at the imperial court. The Tang mural in the Dunhuang Grottoes, *An Outing by the Lady of Song*, shows acrobatics, dancing, singing and horsemanship. At the head of a procession of performers is a man holding an erect pole on which four men are performing stunts, such as climbing the pole, balancing on one's head and hanging upside down. Later, acrobatics and other variety arts gradually lost their preeminence to a new form of entertainment, the opera, and sank to the lowest stratum of society. As variety became a folk art, it absorbed rich nourishment from the lives of ordinary people. This has not only promoted its development but also enriched and enlivened its repertory.

Variety arts in old China had a strongly Chinese flavour. Coming from among the working people, they were inseparably bound to their productive work and daily life. Many traditional variety items actually use labour tools and objects from daily life as props, such as hunters' tridents, sabres, swords, tables, chairs, jars and plates. Some items are based on folk games or sports such as shuttlecock, diabolo, weight lifting and balancing on a bamboo pole.

The variety arts were treated with contempt by the old ruling class and often suppressed. Performers were forced to roam far from home, taking with them only what they could carry. Many risked their lives on dangerous stunts in order to earn a living, and the lack of safety measures often led to fatal accidents among performers of high-flying stunts. Many fine traditional items disappeared altogether, and the 2,000-year-old variety tradition was on the verge of extinction in 1949.

(2) VARIETY ARTS IN NEW CHINA

Since the founding of New China, the people's government has made great efforts to revive and develop traditional Chinese variety arts. Under the policy "let a hundred flowers blossom" and "weed through the old to bring forth the new", Chinese variety arts have been experiencing a renaissance. Performers have a guaranteed livelihood, there has been a fundamental change in their social position, and performances have come in from the street to proper theatres. Variety arts have now become fully respectable stage arts.

The Founding of Variety Troupes The Chinese Variety Troupe, the first state-run company of its kind, was set up in 1950, and similar troupes were soon set up in the provinces and municipalities. The earliest, largest and most famous troupes are the Chinese, Shanghai, Chongqing, Guangzhou Army, Shenyang, and Wuhan troupes. By the end of 1980, there were over 120 state-run companies staffed by a total of over 10,000 performers. Since 1949, these troupes have made great contributions in discovering and re-choreographing good traditional items, creating new ones, training young artists and promoting international cultural exchanges.

Aside from the professional troupes, a great many amateur groups or teams have been set up in factories and villages. With assistance from elderly retired artists and professional troupes, the amateurs have reached fairly high standards. While enriching people's cultural life, these amateur groups and teams also serve as a reservoir of young talents.

New Repertories After the birth of New China, Chinese variety artists investigated, re-choreographed and reformed the traditional variety repertory, discarding dangerous, violent and vulgar items and creating fresh, healthy and beautiful new ones. The rhythm of dance and the movements of callisthenics were incorporated into the new acts, and improvements were made in musical accompaniment and stage design. By 1961, the standard acrobatic repertory had already expanded to 200 items as compared with just a few dozen in 1949, and juggling and conjuring acts increased to over 100.

Traditional items have been made more attractive by improving techniques and adding new stunts. Traditional rope-walking, for example, has now become tight-wire walking, a dazzling display of skill and daring. In the 1950s, the acrobat could only make a forward roll on the rope; today, the performer can make continuous forward rolls, forward and backward somersaults, somersaults from a standing position and exaggerated turnabouts. "Five tables" was formerly a balancing act performed on a pyramid of five tables one on top of the other. Now it has developed into a very skilful and graceful balancing act on a pyramid of 7-10 chairs stacked at an angle, performed by an individual performer, pairs or groups. Plate-spinning artists can now simultaneously spin 12-14 plates, instead of only 4-6 as before, while the performers, usually women, carry out difficult stunts like somersaulting and bending backwards to pick up a flower from the floor in their mouths. Juggling with jars, usually performed by men, has developed from a solo performance with a few ordinary stunts where the performer tosses a jar weighing about eight kilogrammes into the air with one hand, kicks it with his foot, rolls it around his back, spins it round his fingers and balances it on his head, into a dual performance in which the jar is tossed between two men from head to head. Balancing stacks of bowls on the head while making a handstand was improved by the celebrated performer Xia Juhua, who transformed it into a thrilling stunt where she balances the bowls on her head and feet while standing on one hand. On this foundation, all kinds of visually attractive acts have been developed. A traditional form of conjuring known as "ancient splendour" which goes back to the Han Dynasty, "Taking Fish and Dragons for a Stroll" has been brought to a new level in Yang Xiaoting's "Auspicious Abundance". In this act, the performer whose only prop is an embroidered rug around his body produces in turn a score of variously-sized glass bowls filled with water and gold fish, and a blazing metal bowl. Mimicry has increased its range from just over 30 items at the beginning of the fifties to more than 100. Sun Tai and Zhou Zhicheng not only vividly re-create the sounds of singing birds and flying insects but bring to the audience the sounds of winds, waves, crowds, parade drills, musical instruments, weapons and trains.

In addition, many new items have been added to the repertoire, either brand-new creations or adaptations from other activities. These include seesaw stunts, roller skating, balancing gymnastics, bowl balancing from a unicycle (where the performer, seated on a unicycle on a raised platform, uses his foot to flip bowls on to his head) and springboard stunts. All of these new items have reached a fairly high level. On the springboard, for instance, the performer can leap seven metres high, and after making two complete spins, lands on a two-man pyramid. New items are also created by increasing the number of performers by two or more people, as in collective trick-cycling, dual flying tridents, and dual pole stunts, so that both the degree of difficulty and the stage appeal are greatly increased. High-altitude stunts were resumed at the end of the 1950s and the beginning of the 1960s, and many new acts have been added to the repertoire, such as tuck dives, flying leaps, and throwing-and-catching.

During high-altitude performances, safety devices are always used to ensure the safety of the performers.

Clowning has been improved to eliminate vulgarity and develop clever and healthy humour. Clowns are portrayed as honest, naive, clever and optimistic characters. Traditional circus acts including horseback riding and stunts with other performing animals have also improved fairly rapidly. Several different kinds of circus troupes have been formed. Chinese stage magic is a product of many years' integration of foreign and traditional Chinese conjuring and now has a distinctively Chinese style. Since the founding of New China, violent items such as "live target practice", knife swallowing and fire eating have been discarded and replaced by healthy, amusing and educational acts.

Reforms in Stage Design and Musical Accompaniment
In the old society, variety shows were mostly staged in the open air without stage sets or costumes, and the musical accompaniment was crude and simple. Since the founding of New China, when variety shows moved indoors to become a full-fledged stage performance, there has been a marked improvement in the stage design, costume and musical accompaniment. At present, the variety stage commonly uses nylon gauze curtains to filter the light to produce dazzling variations in colour in stage lighting. Simple and elegant sets also enhance the performance. Variety troupes throughout the country have their own orchestras or bands, and music has been specially composed to accompany variety performances. Costumes have also been improved, and wooden props, which are clumsy and heavy, have been replaced by lighter, stronger and more beautiful props made of alloys or fibreglass. The use of microphones has helped mimics

increase their repertory of sounds with dozens of new items. These reforms and improvements have greatly extended the range of Chinese variety shows and raised their artistic level, transforming them into a comprehensive stage art.

Training of Variety Artists The new generation of variety performers are trained in the following ways.

1) Veteran masters take on apprentices who learn their skills as they take part in actual performance (this was the most common practice in the early days after the founding of New China).

2) Children selected on the basis of natural aptitude are sent after intensive basic training courses to variety troupes to perform along with veterans so that they may further polish their skills.

3) Regular training classes and courses in art schools select students on the basis of examinations for five to seven years' formal and systematic training, after which the graduates are sent to troupes as fully qualified performers. Training classes of this kind are mostly attached to variety troupes. The Chinese Variety Troupe and the Chongqing Variety Troupe set up the country's first variety training classes in 1954. The Chinese Variety Troupe has run four such classes and trained more than 180 performers, and the Chongqing Troupe has trained more than 140 in five classes. At present, there are 50 training classes or schools for variety performers in China.

4) Junior variety show teams, of which the most famous are those in Guangzhou, Liaoning, Lüda and Wuhan, provide assistance in training from professional troupes. Some of these junior teams have already performed with striking success.

(3) THE CHINESE VARIETY ARTISTS' ASSOCIATION

Founded in 1981, the Chinese Variety Artists' Association is a voluntary association of performers, directors, musicians, writers, stage designers, researchers, educationalists, editors and organizers of the variety arts. It is responsible for the study of variety arts and the promotion of international exchange in this field. It publishes a journal entitled *Variety Arts*. The president of the association is Xia Juhua.

(4) INTERNATIONAL EXCHANGES

In the past three decades or more, some 30 Chinese variety troupes have toured 100 countries. The Chinese Variety Troupe, the Wuhan Variety Troupe, the Guangzhou Army Variety Troupe, the Chongqing Variety Troupe, the Shenyang Variety Troupe and the Shanghai Variety Troupe have between them made 40 visits abroad, performing in 80 countries.

Many Chinese variety artists have taken part in international variety arts festivals and competitions. Several have won gold or silver medals, such as Xia Juhua for bowl balancing, Sun Tai for mimicry, Meng Lingkuan for juggling with a heavy jar, Jin Yeqin for trick-cycling, and Wang Kuiying, Wang Guiying and Wang Shuying for diabolo play. The traditional Chinese conjurer Yang Xiaoting has been made an honorary member of the International Conjurers' Association.

The Chinese Variety Troupe has helped train performers from the Sudan, Ghana, Tanzania and Egypt and has sent coaches to several countries.

An American magic troupe was invited to tour China in 1981.

These activities have helped international exchange in the variety arts and have enhanced mutual understanding and friendship between the Chinese people and the people of other countries.

文学艺术

《中国手册》编辑委员会编

*

外文出版社出版
(中国北京百万庄路24号)
外文印刷厂印刷
中国国际书店发行
(北京399信箱)
1983年(32开)第一版
编号：(英)17050—178
00175
17—E—1668P